Parenting Your Kids with Grace

Parenting Your Kids
with

Grace

Birth to age 10

Dr. Greg and Lisa Popcak

with Jacob Popcak, MA, and Rachael Isaac, MSW

Our Sunday Visitor
Huntington, Indiana

Nihil Obstat
Msgr. Michael Heintz, Ph.D.
Censor Librorum

Imprimatur
✠ Kevin C. Rhoades
Bishop of Fort Wayne-South Bend
December 2, 2020

The *Nihil Obstat* and *Imprimatur* are official declarations that a book is free from doctrinal or moral error. It is not implied that those who have granted the *Nihil Obstat* and *Imprimatur* agree with the contents, opinions, or statements expressed.

Except where noted, the Scripture citations used in this work are taken from the *New American Bible*, revised edition © 2010, 1991, 1986, 1970 Confraternity of Christian Doctrine, Washington, DC, and are used by permission of the copyright owner. All rights reserved. No part of the New American Bible may be reproduced in any form without permission in writing from the copyright owner.

Every reasonable effort has been made to determine copyright holders of excerpted materials and to secure permissions as needed. If any copyrighted materials have been inadvertently used in this work without proper credit being given in one form or another, please notify Our Sunday Visitor in writing so that future printings of this work may be corrected accordingly.

Our Sunday Visitor Publishing Division, Our Sunday Visitor, Inc., 200 Noll Plaza, Huntington, IN 46750, www.osv.com; 1-800-348-2440

ISBN: 978-1-68192-481-6 (Inventory No. T2363)
1. FAMILY & RELATIONSHIPS—Parenting—General.
2. RELIGION—Christian Life—Family.
3. RELIGION—Christianity—Catholic.

eISBN: 978-1-68192-482-3
LCCN: 2021930054

Cover and interior design: Lindsey Riesen
Cover art: Adobe Stock
Interior art: Jacob Popcak

PRINTED IN THE UNITED STATES OF AMERICA

Contents

Introduction

A Letter from the Authors

The Christian family constitutes a specific revelation
and realization of ecclesial communion, and for this
reason it can and should be called a domestic church.

Catechism of the Catholic Church 2204

"Why aren't children born with an instruction manual?" They are! But we like to say that the manual is written in "Catholic." When we began drafting the first edition of *Parenting with Grace* in 2000, we started with a provocative idea. What if, instead of starting with any prior existing assumptions about the "correct" approach to parenting, we let the Church's theology of family and the human person guide our approach? We began by asking:

- What kind of family life does the Church's theology of family ask us to create?
- What attitudes about life and relationships does the Church ask faithful parents to convey?
- What can biology and the social sciences teach us about the best ways to achieve the goals the Church lays out for faithful families?

The original edition of *Parenting with Grace* was the fruit of this inquiry.

This third edition represents almost twenty years of ongoing reflection and refinement of the answers we originally proposed.

What most made this journey possible were insights drawn from Saint John Paul II's relatively new (at the time) teachings known as the Theology of the Body. The Theology of the Body opened up new avenues of cooperation between theology and the sciences. In effect, the Theology of the Body teaches that *biology is theology*. That is, as we prayerfully reflect on God's design of the body — as revealed by science — we can learn a great deal about God's plan for life and relationships. Although, at the time, many people writing on the Theology of the Body focused on ways Saint John Paul's teachings applied to marriage and sexuality, we found that they applied just as much — if not, in some ways, more — to parenting. Since then, others have joined us in this assertion, including, most notably, Professor Mary Shivanandan of the Pontifical John Paul II Institute for Studies on Marriage and Family in her excellent book, *The Holy Family: Model Not Exception.*

Although Saint John Paul's insights offered a fresh approach to integrating faith and science, his work stands on solid ground in the Catholic intellectual tradition. Saint Thomas Aquinas used to say that there are "two books" — the Bible (the book of God's word) and the "Book of Nature" (i.e., science) — to which Catholics must turn to discover God's plan for anything. God is the author of all truth, discovered and revealed. He created the world (which science studies), and he gave us Scripture. Any authentic approach to studying either theology or science should confirm, not contradict, the findings revealed by either (see *Fides et Ratio*).

In the attempt to articulate a Catholic vision of anything — including parenting — the Church encourages us to be open to the insights that come from harmonizing both theology and science. Any approach that seeks to downplay one or the other is "less Catholic" (or, more accurately, "less consistent with the Catholic intellectual tradition") than one that tries to integrate and harmonize insights from both.

This matters because there are lots of ideas about parenting out there, but not all of them pass muster when examined through this authentically Catholic lens. Some child-rearing advice is based on the assertion that "this is how I was raised and I turned out fine" (whether or not that's really true). Other parenting ideas are based on scientific or quasi-scientific theories that can be difficult to reconcile with Catholic theology. Still other parenting approaches are based on a particular author's idiosyncratic understanding of certain theological or biblical principles that might ignore science altogether. Many of the people promoting these ideas speak with authority and attract a wide following, even among Catholics. But that doesn't mean that their ideas actually represent an authentic Catholic view of anything — much less family life.

Of course, we all have to start somewhere. Everyone uses their own relationship with their parents, family, and friends, as well as the resources with which they are most familiar as the starting point for their parenting careers. And yet the Catholic family isn't primarily a human institution. It's a divine one. United through the sacramental life of the Church, your common, ordinary, crazy family becomes something sacred, a domestic church. By checking our basic assumptions about parenting against both the Church's vision and what science can teach about living out that vision in healthy ways, we can discover God's plan for parenting healthy, godly kids.

This is the approach we've taken in each edition of *Parenting with Grace*. In that vein, we're excited to report that the latest edition of this book includes findings from the Symposium on Catholic Family Life and Spirituality, held in summer 2019. For this truly historic event, our organization, the Pastoral Solutions Institute, worked in conjunction with the Our Sunday Visitor Institute, Holy Cross Family Ministries, and the McGrath Institute for Church Life. We gathered almost fifty theologians, social scientists, pastoral counselors, and family ministry professionals, all of whom are internationally recognized for their work and research on faith and family life. Meeting for several days at the University of Notre Dame, the participants shared research from their respective disciplines, prayed together, and discussed the answers to four critical questions:

1. Are Catholic families called to be different from other families in the way we relate to one another in the home? If so, how?

2. What does an authentic, *family-based approach* to Catholic

spirituality look like in practice?

3. What can the latest research tell us about creating a faithful home and raising faithful kids?

4. How can Catholic families be the outposts of evangelization and positive social change that Catholic teaching says they are meant to be?

The key insights developed in response to these questions are included in this book. That said, you don't have to take our word for it! If you're so inclined, we'd love for you to read the book in which those presentations have been published, *Renewing Catholic Family Life*. By including the research from the symposium in this book, we can confidently say that this latest edition of *Parenting with Grace* offers you the best, most current information both Catholic theology and the social sciences have to offer about raising healthy, happy, godly kids and building strong, grace-filled families.

On a personal note, when the first edition of *Parenting with Grace* came out in 2001, our oldest children were still fairly young. Although we're still actively parenting, we're honored that our oldest children, Jacob and Rachael, are now themselves practicing marriage and family therapists who have a profound love for Christ and deep heart for families. We're even more grateful that the Holy Spirit has called them to join us in promoting a uniquely Catholic vision of family life to a new generation. We're blessed by their contributions and insights.

What we most hope you'll take from this introduction is that whatever choices you make about raising your family — and whether or not you follow our advice in particular — as Catholic parents, we owe it to God and our kids to not just fly by the seat of our pants, casually parenting the way we were parented (good or bad), listening only to those sources that confirm our biases, or following any "expert" that doesn't make an honest effort to reconcile their assertions with both science and the Church's theology of family. Catholic parents certainly aren't obliged to all parent exactly the same way, but we are most definitely obliged to do all that we reasonably can to form our parenting consciences by opening our hearts to both the unique *Catholic* theology of family life (as opposed to secular or Protestant visions of the same) and what science can teach us about the healthiest ways to live out that vision.

The good news? The more you try to do this work in good faith and prayer, the more effective you will become as parents, the more confident you'll feel in your parenting role, and the more peaceful your household will become.

God did write a parenting manual that will enable you to raise great kids, but to read it you have to be willing to leave behind what's familiar and comfortable and go where the truths of both faith and science will lead you. Do not be afraid! With a little effort and openness to God's grace, you'll nail this parenting thing in no time.

Sincerely Yours in Christ,
Dr. Greg and Lisa Popcak,
Jacob Popcak, MA, and Rachael Isaac, MSW

Holy Family, pray for us!

PART ONE

Being a Catholic Parent — What's the Difference?

But he said to me, "My grace is sufficient for you,
for power is made perfect in weakness." I will
rather boast most gladly of my weaknesses, in order
that the power of Christ may dwell with me.

2 Corinthians 12:9

Being a godly parent is a wonderful job, but it's a tough one, too! At its heart, being a Christian mom or dad means embracing the idea that "I don't have all the answers — *and that's OK.*" At Momfidence.org, a ministry we founded to support moms at every age and stage of their parenting journey, one of our most important Momfidence Principles is, *I am proud to be a work in progress.* We base this on the encouragement God gave Saint Paul when he was facing his own struggles (see the quote at the top of this chapter). Many moms and dads really struggle with this idea. Some parents worry about "breaking" their kids. They fret about "not doing everything perfectly" or not following "the rules" (whatever *that* means).

Additionally, because we (the authors) approach parenting through both a practical and theological lens, some readers have even accused us of — in their minds — suggesting that they will be bad people, bad parents, or even bad Catholics if they don't follow our advice to the letter. We want to make it abundantly clear at the start of this book that not only do we not believe this, we have always categorically rejected this perception as ridiculous.

Granted, the Church does, in fact, have a unique and beautiful vision for family life. And, as you will see, it's also true that time-tested research shows that there are certain approaches to parenting that are more consistent with that vision. But no one expects you to perfectly follow every jot and tittle every single moment of every single day. And no one — least of all us — will be judging you if you struggle to apply our suggestions either in whole or in part.

Checking Perfectionism at the Door

We'd also like to offer a gentle challenge to our readers. If you have a tendency toward perfectionism in general, or perfectionistic parenting in particular, we invite you to take a big, deep breath and let that go. Now. And if our gentle encouragement doesn't allow you to let yourself off the hook, then please prayerfully consider getting whatever help you might need to lay down all that guilt and anxiety. Do it for yourself, for your family who needs you, and the God who loves you more than you could possibly measure.

Wherever you might be on the perfectionistic parenting spectrum, every parent needs to remember God's encouragement to Saint Paul that he works through our weakness. God wants to transform you and your child through the healing relationship you are creating together with him. That's why Pope Francis wrote that the Christian family is meant to be a kind of spiritual hospital where we heal the damage sin has done to our ability to love one another as God loves us (cf. *Amoris Laetitia*). None of us is a saint — yet. We all have a lot of healing and growing to do. Parenting is meant to stretch us, to challenge us to love a little bit more every day. But like any other patient in a hospital, you can only do so many treatments in one day before you have to lie down and rest a little. So, be patient with yourself. There is a big difference between letting God stretch you and killing yourself to prove to God, your spouse, your mom, your in-laws, your moms group, or anyone else that you're worthy of approval.

By all means, be serious about being a great Catholic mom or dad — just please don't be scrupulous about it. The fact is, some days are going to be a train wreck. That's simply the nature of the job. Just keep one important qualifier in mind: Even though some days are going to be messier than others, try not to accept "train wreck" as "just the way it's supposed to be in our house all the time." As Pope Francis put it, "The biggest danger in life is a bad spirit of ... saying, 'that's just the way I am.'"

Family life can be messy, but it really isn't supposed to be chaotic all, or even most, of the time. As we mentioned in the introduction, the Church teaches that your home is a domestic church. Part of thinking of your home that way means recognizing that while life can sometimes be crazy, *God wants more* for you and your children. Your home — your domestic church — is meant to be the place where you consecrate the crazy world you live in to God so that he can help you bring a little more order, peace, love, and joy out of the chaos every day. On the days where that just seems like too big a job, focus on doing your best to lean into that vision, trust his grace to multiply your efforts just like his multiplied the loaves and the fishes, and never be afraid to ask for help.

To begin our journey, the next several chapters will explore six ways the Catholic theology of family calls Catholic parents to create a different sort of relationship — a discipleship relationship — with their children. They are ...

1. God is our co-parent.
2. Our families are icons of the Trinity. The love we share in our homes isn't based on any human model — including our families of origin — but rather the self-giving, familial love we find at the heart of God.
3. Our families are domestic churches, and we are called to model ourselves after God's family, the Church.
4. We're on a mission to create communion, serve lives, bless

others, and share Christ in all we do.

5. We turn to the saints for inspiration, guidance, and prayer support.

6. We recognize that parenting is a ministry that's meant to give the world what it needs most: the next generation of loving, godly people.

Are you ready? Let's get started!

CHAPTER 1

The First Difference: God Is Our Co-Parent

By calling God 'Father,' the language of faith ... thus draws on the human experience of parents, who are in a way the first representatives of God for man.

CCC 239

O ur children don't belong to us. They belong to God. God gives his children earthly parents because he wants them to be able to feel *his* love through your body and see his face in your eyes. Christian moms and dads are meant to be the face of God to our kids!

Some parents, rather than being comforted by this, are scared witless. They think, "Don't you know how broken/crazy/tired/stressed/lonely/confused/etc. I am?!? I can't possibly show them God's love all by myself!" The *Catechism of the Catholic Church* recognizes that because we are sinful, we aren't capable of perfectly showing God's face to our kids (see 239). The good news is, you're not supposed to do it all by yourself. God wants to help you. But that might mean learning to pray a little differently than you're used to.

First, it is so important to pray with your spouse every day. Thank God for the gift of your family. Ask God to help you be the parents he created you to be. Ask him for the grace to be generous to each other and your children. Ask him to help you see every part your home life — the joys and the struggles — as another opportunity to fill your hearts with his love and grace. If you haven't made a habit of praying daily as a couple, our book *Praying for (and With) Your Spouse* can help you painlessly learn the steps of creating a lifegiving couple-prayer life.

Second, it's critical to pray with your kids every day — not just at formal prayer time, but all day long. If you're having a good moment, don't forget to pray. Out loud. With your kids. Say something like, "Lord, thank you for letting me enjoy my little ones so much right now!" Similarly, if you're struggling, don't forget to pray. Out loud. With your kids. Say something like, "Lord, I'm kind of losing my mind right now. Please help me love these kids with your love." Regardless of how awkward this might feel at first, the more you do it, the more God will bless you through it. Keep it simple. Keep it short. But pray from your heart and pray all day. Don't run away from your kids to be close to God. Invite God to stand next to you all day as you parent. By all means, do whatever you can to carve out special time for prayer, reflection, and adoration, but don't reserve your faith for "special times." Talk to God as if he were another family member standing right next to you and waiting to lend a hand. Because he is!

One tip we discuss in our book *Discovering God Together: The Catholic Guide to Raising Faithful Kids* is to teach your kids to pray over you. We regularly give our kids blessings by laying our hands on them and asking for God's grace for the day, or before special moments (like a test, game, or performance), or when they're hurting physically or emotionally. Once you've modeled this practice, you can also ask your kids to pray over you. We can't tell you how healing it is to be able to call your kids over and say, "Mom/Dad is having a hard day, guys. Can you please pray over me?" and have your 4-year-old put his hand on your knee and say, "Jesus, please help Mommy feel better." Or even, "Please help me be good for Daddy." In the Popcak household, our children have been praying over us their whole lives — just as we have been praying over them all of theirs. Teaching them to pray over you acquaints them with the spiritual power they've been given in baptism as sons and daughters of God. It also reminds them that when *we're* driving *them* crazy (hey, it happens), they can go over our heads and talk to their heavenly Father, secure in the knowledge that he will help them out.

Of course, it's also good to create a little space every day for family prayer time. Dinnertime or bedtime is a good time for many families, but you can do what works best for you. There are many different formats you can use for family prayer. One we developed uses the acronym **PRAISE**. This stands for:

Praise and thanksgiving — Take turns acknowledging the blessings of the day.

Repentance — Take turns asking God for the grace to handle different challenges you faced today better the next time.

Ask for your needs — Take turns asking for God's help with special intentions.

Intercede for others — Take turns asking God to bless those who need our prayers.

Seek his will — Bring all the decisions your family faces to God and ask for his wisdom to help you make the right choices so you can be the family he wants you to be.

Express your desire to keep listening — As you wrap up, ask God for the grace to keep listening to his voice speaking to you through the events of the day so that you can continue to hear him until you meet together again in prayer.

Every family should feel free to tailor this format to their needs, integrating spontaneous or more formal prayers as you see fit. Our template allows you to create a meaningful family prayer ritual that "covers the bases" while still letting you customize it to your family's needs. It can take as little as five minutes or as long as you like depending upon the time you have.

Another great resource for family prayer is the *Household Book of Blessings* published by the United States Conference of Catholic Bishops. It's a great book filled with family prayers and blessings for all occasions.

Of course, as Catholics we don't just enjoy the spiritual communion with Christ that prayer can facilitate. We experience Jesus "up close and personal" through the Eucharist. Human parents often say that their children are their "very own flesh and blood." Through Communion, we literally become God's very own flesh and blood. His Precious Body becomes one with our flesh, and his Precious Blood courses through our veins.

As the old church-camp song says, there is "wonder-working power in the precious blood of the Lamb." Teach your children that as much as you love them, God loves them more. Teach that the Eucharist makes them God's sons and daughters even more than they're yours. We highly encourage regular Eucharistic adoration for families. Remember what Jesus said, "Let the children come to me" (Mt 19:14). There are many ways to do this, of course, but one way we highly recommend is a wonderful program called ChildrenOfHope.org that makes Eucharistic adoration accessible to even preschool children.

The power of the sacraments shouldn't be underestimated. A friend of ours shared this story about how his relationship with Christ in the Eucharist helped him when his parents and teachers couldn't:

> When I was a child, I came to have a really special connection to Jesus in the Eucharist. My parents were great. They shared their deep love of God with me in lots of different ways — especially in the way we prayed together and celebrated the sacraments regularly.
>
> They also sacrificed a lot to send me to Catholic school. Unfortunately, that was an awful experience because I was bullied mercilessly. Neither my teachers or parents were able to help. It got so bad, by junior high, I thought about killing myself. I was so miserable.
>
> Eventually, I started sneaking into the church across the playground during recess. At first, it was just to get away from the bullies, but in time I came to feel that God was calling me to him and holding me in his arms. I felt loved and protected in his presence. I would bring my concerns to him. I would pray for God to help me deal with the kids at school. He did that by giving me a real sense of how loved and precious I was in his eyes. Sometimes I even got in trouble for "hiding out" in church during recess. I guess the teachers thought I was up to some-

thing. I didn't care. God's love was the only thing that got me through those years. I wouldn't wish my grade-school experience on anyone, but I wouldn't give up that time I spent in God's presence for anything. The graces I received there helped me be the man I am today as much as anything my parents ever did — and they did a lot.

In sum, pray with your kids. Pray over your kids. Teach them to pray over you. Help them experience God's love in a personal way through all the sacraments. Teach them to think of God as the person who knows them best and loves them most. Just remember that all day, every day, God wants to parent alongside you and to fill in whatever gaps even your best efforts to love your kids will inevitably leave behind.

Prayer

Lord, help me to remember that my children are your children first and that you want to parent with me. Please come into every moment of my parenting life. Let me remember to lead my children in thanking you for the good times and asking you for help in the difficult times. Help me to experience your love more deeply in the Eucharist and to bring the love I find there home to my family. Help me lean more on the love, mercy, patience, joy, and strength that flows from your heart — especially when my own runs dry. Make me the parent you want me to be so that when my children look into my eyes, they will always see your loving face smiling back at them.

Holy Family, pray for us. Amen.

Questions for Discussion

What practical difference would it make to behave as if God were parenting alongside you all day long?

What specific parenting challenges would you like to ask God's help with? How could you invite God into those moments when they are happening? What difference would it make for you to do so?

What ideas from this chapter would you like to start practicing today? How could you tailor these suggestions to your family?

CHAPTER 2

The Second Difference: Your Family Is an Icon of the Trinity

The primordial model of the family is to be sought in
God himself, in the Trinitarian mystery of his life.

Pope Saint John Paul II, Letter to Families

The Christian family is a communion of persons,
a sign and image of the communion of the
Father and the Son in the Holy Spirit.

CCC 2205

The more we pray, especially when we pray in the honest, heartfelt manner we discussed in the last chapter, the more we reveal our inner life, our hopes, dreams, fears, and desires, to God. But because prayer is a conversation, the more we pray, the more God also reveals something about his inner life to us.

One of the things God has revealed to the Church about his inner life is that, in his very nature, *he is a family.* God is one God, but three persons, Father, Son, and Holy Spirit. The love that exists between the three Persons of the Trinity is familial. As Saint John Paul put it, "God in his deepest mystery is not a solitude [i.e., an individual], but a family, since he has in himself fatherhood, sonship and the essence of the family, which is love."[1]

There's an important lesson in this for parents. We know God created us in his "image and likeness," but that doesn't only refer to us as individual persons. God also created the human family in his image and likeness so that when people see the way Christian families love one another, they might get a little peek at what God's love looks like. That's why the Church calls Christian families "icons of the Trinity."[2]

The Challenge of Love

As you can imagine, there's a lot to unpack here. Entire books have been written on the subject, and we're not even going to attempt to scratch the surface about what all this theology means. But on a very practical level, one important takeaway for parents is that God calls Christian families to model themselves after him and the love that lives at his heart.

When spouses argue about parenting, they usually do so because "your family showed love in one way and my family showed love in another way." As a Christian, the love you experienced in your family of origin is less important than the love God has in his heart for you and your kids. That's the love he wants us to learn to share with one another, little by little, day by day. God doesn't want us to show our family of origin's face to the world. He wants our families to show his face to the world. We must decrease so God may increase (Jn 3:30).

Hopefully our families of origin showed us God's love at least to some degree. But whether or not they succeeded, it's our mission as Christian families to exemplify God's love more than any human model we've encountered. That's a tall order, and more often than not, we're going to fail miserably. That's OK. The point isn't to do this perfectly. The point is to remember that God wants to fill our hearts with a love that's bigger than anything we've ever experienced, and he wants us to do our best to pass that love on to our kids — *his kids* — too.

We all love our kids, but because we are sinful and broken, we are sometimes afraid to love our kids as much as God wants us to. That's a perfectly natural struggle, but as Catholic parents, it's not our place to decide how much love we're going to give our kids. Because we are his face, God wants us to love our children — as much as we possibly can — with the generous, passionate, joyful, self-giving love that flows from his heart. That's how we become saints, after all. Saints are simply people who have mastered the art of letting God's love shine out in their lives. In this sense, Catholic families are meant to be saint-making machines, inviting one another to use all the stuff of everyday life to learn how to love one another with God's love — one diaper change, one baby step, one runny nose, one homework assignment, one game night at a time.

The Big Question

If any of this seems overwhelming, remember Saint John Paul's admonition, "Be not afraid!" You're not alone. God wants to do this with you. The best way to start sharing the love that comes from the heart of the Trinity with your children is to prayerfully reflect on the following question every day:

> Given *both* the very real strengths *and* the very real limitations I'm dealing with, what's *one small thing I could do right now* to narrow the gap between the love/patience/compassion/generosity/mercy I'm naturally equipped to give my kids and the love/patience/compassion/generosity/mercy God wants to give my kids through me?

Don't try to do this on your own power. Pray for the grace to make this happen. Get the support of your spouse, your family, your faith community, a spiritual director, or even a professional therapist when necessary. But don't forget that Catholic parents are called to more than worldly parents are. No matter how great your family of origin was, it isn't enough to raise your kids the way you were raised. We're called to create families that are icons of the Trinity by allowing our hearts to be filled with God's love and then generously sharing that love with our spouse and children. If there is anything standing in the way of our ability to do that, we're *obliged* as disciples of Christ to get whatever help we need to remove the obstacles so that our households can be the conduits of love that they are meant to be.

Prayer

Lord, let my family be a true "icon of the Trinity": a home that radiates the love that comes from your heart inside and out. Help me to never settle for anything less than the love you want to give me and to never share anything less with my children than the love you want to give them through me. Give me the grace to use every moment of my parenting day as an opportunity to learn how to trade my human love for your godly love. Let me be patient with myself when I struggle or fail, but let me always keep this vision in mind so that even on my toughest, most imperfect days, I can remember to wrap them up in your arms and look at them through your eyes.

Holy Family, pray for us! Amen.

Questions for Discussion

What practical difference does it make to think of your family as an "icon of the Trinity"?

In what ways did your family of origin reflect the generous, abundant, merciful love that is found at the heart of the Trinity? In what ways did they struggle to do this? Practically speaking, how do you think God is calling you to give more of his love to your children than your parents were able to give to you?

Name one challenge you face in your relationship with your kids, in which you'd like to do a better job of loving them with God's love. What would that more loving difference look like in practice?

CHAPTER 3

The Third Difference: Your Family Is Part of God's Family

"The Father ... determined to call together in a holy Church those who should believe in Christ." This "family of God" is gradually formed and takes shape during the stages of human history, in keeping with the Father's plan.

CCC 759

"The Christian family constitutes a specific revelation and realization of ecclesial communion, and for this reason it can and should be called a domestic church." It is a community of faith, hope, and charity; it assumes singular importance in the Church.

CCC 2204

Most people have no idea how important family life is to God. So far, we've seen that God is like a family in his very nature, and that he created human families to live in his image. In this chapter, we'll look at how he created his own earthly family, the Church, to serve as a model for how Christian families are called to relate to one another.

The Catholic Church isn't just another membership club. Catholics believe that the Church is, literally, God's family. Your domestic church, your household, is a branch of this divine family tree. The theme of family runs through every aspect of the sacramental life of the Church. For example:

- We're born into God's family through the baptismal font — which is literally considered the womb of the Church.
- The Eucharist is the family meal that God prepares for his children so that we might live forever.
- Confirmation initiates Christians into God's "family business": building the kingdom of God and bringing the world to Christ.

These are just a few examples.

From the beginning of time, God intended the human family to play a starring role in revealing his face to the world. Unfortunately, after the Fall, sin damaged the love and order God intended human families to live in. The world needed a model of the kind of family life God wants all of his children to experience. So, God sent his Son to establish the Church as his family on earth. By seeing how God "parents" his children through the Church, his children can learn to be godly families again.

The Catholic theology of family suggests that Catholic households should take our cues for how we relate to one another from the way God relates to us through his family, the Church. That's one of the deeper senses in which "the Church is a family of families."[1] As a "domestic church" your family is meant to be a "chip off the old block," so to speak. A little outpost of God's family in the world.

What can God's family, the Church, teach us about parenting? Lots! In this chapter, we'll explore five specific lessons we can learn by following the Church's example.

1. Connection is key
2. The sacred power of family meals

3. Self-donation is the key to obedience
4. Combine high standards with gentle discipline
5. Your home life is a liturgy

God's Family Tip #1: Connection is key

If Christ had not first responded to our cries, become one of us, and gathered us to him, there would not have ever been a Church to begin with. Before God could make us his family, he had to gather us together in his love. He had to make a real connection with us and *attach himself to us* — and us to him — in a real and embodied way. He emptied himself and became one of us. He taught us. He healed us. He ate with us. He lived and worked and laughed and cried with us. Ultimately, he suffered, died, and rose for us. But Jesus Christ didn't just do all that way back when. The sacraments are God's family rituals that make Christ present to us today. Through these powerful God-given rituals of connection, God continues to gather his family together, teaches us how to live in communion, forgives us when we fail, shows us how to do better, and gives us the love, nourishment, and support we need to become whole, healed, healthy, godly persons — just like he wants earthly families to do.

Following the example of God's family, the Church, Catholic parents are invited to make our domestic churches places that foster real communion by establishing and protecting strong family rituals. Just like God's family is intentional about prioritizing the rituals that bring order to God's "house" (our parish church), Catholic parents should be intentional about creating strong family rituals that enable us to experience love, peace, grace, and joy in our households. Having regular rituals that enable your family to work, play, talk, and pray together at least a few minutes every day is critical to making your home a dynamic and soul-satisfying domestic church.

Rituals aren't just nice things families do once in a while. They are regular, intentional, planned (and, mostly, obligatory) times where families gather to work, play, talk, and pray together:

- Examples of simple, daily *work rituals* include things like clearing the table together or cleaning up the kitchen as a family after meals, picking up the family room together before bed, folding laundry, or making beds together.

- Examples of simple, daily *play rituals* include things like taking a walk together, playing a board game or card game together, working on a craft project or puzzle, or reading aloud.

- Examples of simple, daily *talk rituals* include discussing the highs and lows of the day over dinner or before bed, family meetings, and regular one-on-one time with a parent.

- Examples of simple, daily *prayer rituals* could include any of the things we discussed in the earlier chapters on praying together or any other type of prayer that helps you draw closer to God and each other.

If you made a commitment to do at least one thing every day to work, play, talk, and pray together as a family, it might take a total of forty-five to sixty minutes combined, but we guarantee it would change your life. And these are more than just nice things to do. Godly families that regularly work, play, talk, and pray together model the relationships Christians are meant to have to work, leisure, relationships, and God. In a Catholic household, family rituals are a catechism in Christian living.

Almost sixty years of research show that the better established a family's rituals are, the more likely it is that they will be happy, stable, and close.[2] The same body of research shows that the more intentional a family is about creating rituals for working, talking, and praying and playing together, the easier it is for parents to pass on their faith and values to their kids — without having to resort to lecturing and nagging. We'll talk more about how you can create meaningful family rituals throughout this book. For now, it's enough to know that God's family, the Church, asks us to participate in so many rituals because they help us be happier, healthier people. They create a strong sense of identity and community, and they reinforce all the lessons God wants to teach his children about living a grace-filled life. They teach us how to relate, as Christian persons, to all the activities that make us fully human.

God's Family Tip #2: The sacred power of family meals
Speaking of meaningful rituals, the single most meaningful ritual God's

family celebrates is the regular "family meal" we call the Eucharist. Through that meal, we learn that God is a hands-on parent. Any time we call on him, he takes time out of the busiest schedule in the universe to be there — body, blood, soul, and divinity.

Of course, the Eucharist isn't just some symbol. It's the actual Body and Blood of Christ. The Eucharist is the way God creates communion with his children. Inspired by the example of God's family, Catholic families are encouraged to celebrate meaningful family meals as a way of creating a sense of communion in the home. Pope Francis asserted the importance of meaningful family meals when he said, "A family that almost never eats together, or that never speaks at the table but looks at the television or the smartphone, is hardly a family."[3]

Mealtimes in the domestic church are meant to be a kind of sacred event. We don't mean they're sacred because they somehow involve holy water, perfect manners, good china, classical music, and locally sourced, organic produce. In fact, they're probably even more sacred when they're messy and noisy and simple. What makes family mealtimes a sacred event in your domestic church isn't all the trappings; it's that they are opportunities to share *yourselves* with one another, especially if you make a point of discussing topics that don't come up naturally, like the high and low points in the day, how you can better love and support one another that day, and what God might be trying to communicate to you (both individually and as a family) through the events of your day. By doing these things, you create real communion in your domestic churches, which feeds your family's soul. Making a regular, meaningful family meal happen can be challenging, but it's an important way that Catholic families say to one another, "Other than God, you are the most important thing in the world to me. I promise to make the time to show you that every day at this meal."

God's Family Tip #3: Self-donation is the key to obedience

Through the sacraments we discover that God "commands" his children's obedience, not by bossing us around or scaring us into submission, but by giving us so much of himself that we can't help but want to draw closer to him. Even when sin makes us want to resist his love, he continues to give himself to us. Like a father who gently holds a fussy child until he melts — reluctantly but inevitably — into his loving embrace, God holds us in his arms until our tantrumming stops, our angry, pouting hearts melt, and we let him lead us.

"Self-giving" (also "self-donation") is a phrase that appears time and again in Saint John Paul II's writings. It means that just as God is immeasurably generous to us, he wants us to use everything he has given us — our time, treasure, talent, and even our bodies — to work for the good of the people he has placed in our life, starting with our spouse and children. Even though doing this sometimes feels hard, finding the courage to do it anyway is the key to becoming both happy and holy. As the Church says, we find ourselves by making a gift of ourselves.[4]

As you saw above, the Eucharist is a self-giving meal. It represents the most important way — out of a zillion other ways — that God gives all of himself to us and invites us to give all of ourselves back to him. Through this self-giving sacrament, God makes us want to offer our obedience freely to him as a loving response to the love he first gives us.

This is the model of discipline God wants human parents to use. Discipline rooted in a self-giving relationship with our kids makes true obedience possible. Instead of requiring us to settle for the compliance we can command out of fear, discipline rooted in a self-giving relationship enables us to capture our children's hearts and form them in love. In his Theology of the Body, Saint John Paul made an important distinction between a moral ethos (where you do what is right out of love) versus a moral ethic (where you do what's right out of fear). This is an important distinction for parents. Would you rather your kids behave out of a genuine love for you and desire to please you (moral ethos) or because they were simply afraid of getting caught doing something wrong (moral ethic)? In many ways, the source of our obedience matters even more than obedience itself.

Responding to our baby's cries promptly, making the effort to give children of every age extravagant affection, gently correcting and guiding them, playing with them, and giving them our time and attention can be very hard sometimes, but these simple practices become the way Catholic parents follow the self-giving approach to parenting God models through the sacraments in his family, the Church. They are the ways parents lay the foundation for a moral ethos in our children — a bone-deep desire to do what's right because it is the loving thing to do.

Both Saint John Paul's Theology of the Body and the science of neurology[5] teach us that human beings are literally wired to defer to those who make us feel cared for. It isn't just our mind that responds this way. Our body does too. For instance, scientists tell us hugs feel good because they allow the calmer person to, in a sense, "download" their emotional state into the more stressed-out person.[6] Hugs sync up the embracing couple's heartrate, respiration, and body temperature. The sigh you give when you get a really good hug means "Download complete. My body is now synced up with yours." That's what feeling connected to someone means. When we feel truly cared for, every part of us — our mind, body, and spirit — wants to "listen" and learn from the person who is giving themselves to us.

This is an important lesson for parents. You can force a child to do your will, but as soon as your back is turned, that child will most likely look for ways to rebel against your authority. If you really want to command someone's heart — especially a child's — being authentically self-giving is the only way to go.

This is exactly how God parents us. Parents follow the heavenly Father's example best when we take time to *listen* to our children — not just with our ears, but with our whole selves — so that we can understand the needs and concerns on their hearts and help them address those needs and concerns in godly, fulfilling ways. The parent who does this commands their child's obedience without having to threaten or bribe. Children raised by genuinely self-giving parents learn the unconscious lesson that, "when I listen to Mom and/or Dad, they help me meet my needs in ways that not only make me happy, but also help me feel better about myself." Their obedience is easier to command because they want to willingly give it as a loving response to you having loved them first.

God's Family Tip #4: Combine high standards with gentle discipline

God's family, the Church, offers Catholic parents another parenting tip in the form of the Sacrament of Reconciliation. On the one hand, the members of God's family are held to tremendously high standards. God actually wants us to be saints! On the other hand, God is a tremendously gentle disciplinarian. Those "five Hail Mary" penances are not meant to punish us. They are meant to be an opportunity to step into the role of the Prodigal Son (see Lk 15:11–32), to be held in the Father's arms where we can experience a love so powerful that it makes us never want to leave home again.

Later in this book, we'll explore how you can have even higher standards for your little ones' behavior employing loving-guidance methods rather than heavy-handed punishments. For now, it's enough to know that if our heavenly Father can nudge us along the road to sainthood without losing his patience, maybe — just maybe — he can show us some tricks for getting our kids to pick up their socks without having to lose our minds.

God's Family Tip #5: Your home life is a liturgy

There is one final, critical lesson we can learn about parenting from God's family, the Church. Namely, the more we try to parent our children as God the Father parents us, the more our family life, itself, becomes a *liturgy*.

"Liturgy" is a word that refers to the way God "works" through his family, the Church, to heal the damage sin has done to our relationships with him and one another. The Liturgy of the Eucharist (i.e., Mass) restores our union with God and makes communion with others possible. In a complementary way, the Liturgy of Domestic Church Life enables you to bring Jesus home after you receive him so that he can continue to heal the damage sin has done to the relationships in your family and your world. Similar to the way that ordained priests preside over the Liturgy of the Eucharist, you could say that, through the common priesthood we received at baptism, Catholic parents preside over the Liturgy of Domestic Church Life. By seeking the grace to love each other with Christ's sacrificial love, Catholic moms and dads consecrate all the mundane aspects of family life and enable Christ to make them holy.

Do you know all those days where you feel like "what's the point?" Those days when the toys won't stay put away and the kids are driving you crazy and all you want to do is run away and find something "important" to do? Realizing that your family *isn't* just a never-ending to-do list, but an actual living, breathing, domestic church that God wants to use to show you his love, make you holy, and help your kids be loved and holy too, stops you from simply living in survival mode. It reminds us that it's possible to thrive as parents — emotionally, relationally, and spiritually — because God's grace is hiding behind every runny nose, every silly giggle, every skinned knee, and every tearful face. Instead of just white-knuckling your way through the next hassle that family life throws at you, remembering that, through it all, you are celebrating the Liturgy of Domestic Church Life enables you to see that God is using every part of your parenting day — all those sleepless nights, frustrating experiences, and joyful moments — to help you do a better job of both receiving his love and sharing it with the children he has placed in your care.

All of the things you do to parent your kids and create a loving home aren't just "stuff you have to do." Changing diapers, picking up after your kids, preparing family meals, forming your rug rats into godly human beings, and all the rest become the means by which God perfects *you* in grace as well as giving your kids a visible sign of how much God loves them. Celebrating the Liturgy of Domestic Church Life in your domestic church makes everything you do as a parent sacred and sacramental. By doing these things with God's love in mind, the Liturgy of Domestic Church Life heals the damage sin has done (and wants to do) to your family.

As a Catholic family you are truly blessed to live a different vision of family life than you can find anywhere else in the world. Your household isn't just a boring little place where boring little dramas are played out day in and day out. Your home is a divine institution, created by God to be an outpost of grace in the world. Your domestic church is a place where you and yours can be filled with the all-consuming, transforming love of God who cares about you so much that there isn't any single part of your life that he doesn't want to be involved in — especially the most boring and frustrating parts. And all you have to do is follow the Church's example to find grace hidden where you'd least expect it.

Prayer

Lord, help me to model my domestic church after your family, the Church. Help us to create strong rituals that bind us together in love. Help me to communicate my expectations for my children's behavior clearly, but guide them gently. Let me "command" their obedience, not by the force of my will, but through the power of your love. And help me to celebrate the Liturgy of Domestic Church Life in a way that enables me to encounter your grace hiding just below the surface of everything we do to maintain our home and create a strong family life.

Holy Family, pray for us! Amen.

Questions for Discussion

What rituals did you have as a family growing up? How did they bring you closer? What rituals for working, playing, talking, and praying together as a family do you have in your domestic church? How might you strengthen or build on them?

What does it mean for you to think of Christian obedience, not as a response to being forced or compelled to do something, but as a loving response to being loved? How might this idea challenge you to think differently about the way you "command" obedience from your children?

What practical difference does it make to think about your family life as a Liturgy of Domestic Church Life that is intended to help you live the grace of the Eucharist at home and heal the damage sin has done to the relationships in your home?

CHAPTER 4

The Fourth Difference: We're on a Mission from God

*The family finds in the plan of God the Creator and Redeemer
not only its identity, what it is, but also its mission, what
it can and should do. ... Hence the family has the mission
to guard, reveal and communicate love, and this is a living
reflection of and a real sharing in God's love for humanity
and the love of Christ the Lord for the Church His bride.*

Pope Saint John Paul II, *Familiaris Consortio,* 17

As domestic churches, Catholic families are called to share in the "life and mission of the Church."[1] As far as the Church is concerned, every Catholic family is on a mission from God. When we do it intentionally and prayerfully, family life is a real, honest-to-goodness *ministry* that can transform hearts, make the world a better place to live, and call others to Christ. Although we usually think of "ministry" as "the churchy things we do at church," in reality "ministry" is any activity we engage in that conveys God's love to another person. If that doesn't describe Catholic family life, we don't know what does.

Saint John Paul II taught that your domestic church builds up the kingdom of God by committing to four critical tasks:

1. Create a deep, loving, and intimate communion in the home.
2. Serve life, both through our openness to having children and by diligently working to help the children we have be godly people at every age and stage.
3. Be a blessing to others, both through the witness of our life as a family and through our service to our parish and community.
4. Share Christ with others, both through our faithful example as a family and through our mutual commitment to living the life and mission of the Church.

1. Create a deep, loving, and intimate communion in the home

Catholic parents respond to the Church's call to create deep, loving, and intimate communion in our homes both by making affection and connection job number one and by helping our kids experience the Faith as the source of the warmth in our home.[2] Research shows us that practices like extravagant affection, loving-guidance approaches to discipline, and prompt, generous, and consistent responses to our children's needs are the best ways faithful parents can connect their children's hearts to the heart of God.[3]

The world says that work, school, and extracurricular activities come first, and you fit family life in … if you can. *The Church* asks us to treat family time as the most important appointment in our week and to commit to other activities only to the degree that they don't stop us from truly connecting with our spouse and children. As Pope Francis put it, one of the most important things parents can do to build the kingdom of God is to "waste time" with your children.[4]

2. Serve life, both through our openness to having children and by diligently working to help the children we have be godly people at every age and stage

Catholic parents' commitment to serve life essentially involves two things. First, that you and your spouse would ask God every day to make you open to the children he wants to give you — whether that means that your family may ultimately be either bigger or smaller than you, yourself, envisioned. Second, that you and your spouse ask God every day to help you give your children everything they need to grow up to be healthy, godly men and women who can glorify him with their lives. Balancing these two goals stands at the heart of what the Church calls "responsible parenthood" — that is, cultivating an openness to life that is respectful of the need to raise fully formed, godly persons. Each day, we should sit down *with our spouse* and offer a prayer that goes something like this:

> Lord, we give our hearts and our family to you. Help us to be open to having the children you want to give us. And help us raise the children we have in your love, so that they may come to know you and never depart from you. Make us the family you want us to be.

Remember, our family belongs to God. If we truly want to be a godly family, we have to regularly ask him what he wants for us. Of course, we have a say in how it all works out. In fact, we have quite a lot of say. God, in his mercy, is deeply respectful of our needs, concerns, strengths, and limitations. Moreover, he wants *us* to be respectful of our needs, concerns, strengths, and limitations — because we will struggle to raise godly kids if we aren't (see chapter nine). Children are certainly a great blessing from the Lord (see Ps 127:4–5), but the most important thing for Catholics is not the number of children we have. Rather, it is doing our best to provide all the children God gives us with everything they need to be godly adults. "For one can be better than a thousand; rather die childless than have impious children!" (Sir 16:3).

Ultimately, God knows us best and loves us most. The call to serve life is a call to prayerfully discerning God's vision for both our family size and family dynamic. In this way, we can discover how to build a domestic church that glorifies God and fully respects our unique strengths and struggles.

3. Be a blessing to others, both through the witness of our life as a family and through our service to our parish and community

We live in a hurting world. As domestic churches, we don't just live for ourselves. We're called to share God's love with the world in whatever ways make sense based upon our family's current state in life.

As important as giving back truly is, with a little creativity, you don't necessarily even have to leave home to make a difference. In fact, in some ways, it's better if you don't. Pope Francis cautioned parents against becoming so busy — whether at work or service — that they turn their children into "orphans, but within the family."[5] There are lots of ways your family can serve others without even leaving the house. The website DoingGoodTogether.org offers many suggestions for family service in the home and in the community.

That said, a word of caution is in order. We've encountered many well-meaning, faithful parents who thought that if they just dedicated their lives to serving others — even if it meant sacrificing strong family rituals and an intimate home life — their kids would learn the importance of Christian service. More often what happens is that kids become resentful. While serving others is important, when parents only seem to care for people with problems, our kids can begin to think they must become people with problems in order to get us to care about them.

The good news is that there are about a bazillion-and-one ways your family can work *together* to be a blessing to others and simultaneously develop a stronger relationship with your kids. We'll explore more ways to do this throughout the book.

4. Share Christ with others, both through our faithful example as a family and through our mutual commitment to living the life and mission of the Church

You probably know any number of people — friends, extended family members, coworkers — who would most likely never darken the door of a church. How are you sharing Jesus with them?

Don't let this question intimidate you. Sharing Christ with others doesn't have to be an onerous or even deeply religious task. For instance, at the Symposium for Catholic Family Life and Spirituality, Pat Fagan, the director of the Marriage and Religion Research Institute (Marri.us), said that he wished every Catholic family would host an annual barbecue/block party for their neighbors. They wouldn't have to do anything except be hospitable, give everyone a chance to get to know one another better, and provide some wholesome games or entertainment. The only religious thing they would need to do was offer a thoughtful, heartfelt prayer of blessing before the meal.

He imagined that the host family wouldn't see any fruit right away. Maybe even for years. But one day, out of the blue, the husband or wife would hear from a neighbor who would say, "Listen, you're, like, a Christian, right? Can I ask you something?" It might be a question about their marriage, or their kids, or some faith topic, or anything at all. But now the door is open, and the Catholic family barely had to do anything. At the very least, the Catholic family on the block would establish themselves as caring people who wanted to bring others together. That's two-thirds of what good evangelization involves.

Think of how the world would change if every Catholic family on the planet did just this much. And that's only one idea. In *Discovering God Together: The Catholic Guide to Raising Faithful Kids*, we offer a ton of great tips for how your family can bring Christ to the world through your example of love.

Your Family Mission and Charism

Finally, a simple way you can enhance your family's ability to effectively practice the four critical tasks is to discern your family's mission and charism. A family mission helps you identify the qualities God wants your family to practice to live a more abundant life together. A family charism clarifies the ways your family can use the gifts and talents God gave you to be a blessing to others.

Family Mission

God didn't bring you together by accident! He created your family so that you could build the kingdom in a special way that's unique to you.

Although each person in your family is different, you share a life in common. Because of that, there are probably some virtues (like respect, joy, love, justice, mercy, generosity, peace, compassion, etc.) that would be of special importance in your house. Likewise, as a family, you may have certain interests, talents, or skills (e.g., music, sports, arts and crafts, teaching, service, hospitality, organization, etc.) in common.

To determine your family mission, pray as a family over time about the qualities or virtues that you think are most important to living a good, godly life together. As you think about the different personalities in your home, what are the virtues you need to practice most to create a loving, joyful, faithful, orderly family? Below are some examples of some virtues that could be the basis of your family mission. Feel free to come up with others that fit your family life more accurately. Choose three to four qualities/virtues that will be the foundation of your family mission.

Love	Generosity	Compassion
Service	Respect	Peace
Joy	Kindness	Self-Control
Patience	Faith	Wisdom
Prudence	Doing Right	Life Balance

List others here: _____

_____

Now organize these qualities in the form of a family mission statement.

> We are the (Name) family. We have been called together by God
> to live lives of (insert qualities here) in our relationships with
> one another and everyone we meet.

Review this mission statement regularly over family meals or in family meetings. Reflect on what you are doing to live out these qualities in the way you relate to one another, your decisions as a family, and your interactions with others. Ask one another what you could do to be better examples of these qualities in your personal lives and in your life as a family. Consider these qualities in the decisions you make. What choices would help you do a better job of living out these virtues? What choices would make it more difficult?

Over time, continue to pray about your family mission. Is God asking you to practice different virtues as your circumstances change? Let your family mission statement draw you together to strengthen your family and build the kingdom of God in your own unique way.

Family Charism

To discern your family charism, prayerfully reflect on gifts, talents, or interests you share in your family. Examples include things like sports, music, art, performing, hospitality, service, hard work, building, creating, teaching, leading, helping, etc. List these below.

God has blessed our family with the following gifts, talents, and interests:

_____

_____

_____

Now, as a family, prayerfully reflect on the question, *How can we bless others with the gifts, talents, or interests we share?* You might have certain gifts, talents, or interests in common, or you might see creative ways to combine the different individual gifts, talents, or interests you have. The answer to this question provides insights into the charisms you have been given. A charism is more than a gift, talent, or interest. It is a gift, talent, or interest that is consecrated to God and used to bless the Body of Christ.

Just as God calls different religious orders (Franciscans, Jesuits, Benedictines, Salesians, etc.) to bless the world with their unique missions and charisms, every domestic church is called together by God to serve his kingdom in some unique way. Your family has every bit as important a part to play in building the kingdom of God as any "official" religious order. As the *Catechism* puts it, "The Christian family constitutes a specific revelation and realization of ecclesial communion" (2204). Whether you realize it or not, your Catholic household is meant to be a bona fide ministry and outreach of the Church. Discerning your family mission and charism enables you to deepen your understanding of all the ways God wants to use your household to be a blessing to the world!

Conclusion

Don't ever feel that you aren't doing great things for the kingdom because you're busy paying bills, changing diapers, and trying not to step on LEGOs. All of these simple activities are part of the Liturgy of Domestic Church Life that, done lovingly and prayerfully, enable you to be outposts of God's love in the world. By doing the best you can to live out the four critical tasks and discern your family mission and charism, your family becomes a true ministry, equipped by God's grace to communicate his love to the world and participate in his plan to heal the damage sin has done to all of our relationships.

Prayer

Lord, help my family, my domestic church, be mindful of our mission to create an intimate communion in our home, to raise each child you give us to love you with all their hearts, to be a blessing to those in need, and to bring Christ to everyone we know. Make us your outposts of love and grace in the world so that through our witness, we can draw the whole world to you.

Holy Family, pray for us! Amen.

Questions for Discussion

How did your family of origin live out the fourfold mission of a Catholic family (Create Communion, Serve Life, Be a Blessing, Share Christ)? Would you want your parents' example to impact the way you and your children live out this fourfold mission? If so, how?

In what ways does your domestic church already live out the fourfold mission of Catholic families (whether intentionally or not)? What is one thing you could do to live each of the four missions more intentionally?

How do you think identifying your family mission or charism would help you experience God's grace more fully or serve others more effectively?

CHAPTER 5

The Fifth Difference: We Aren't Too Proud to Listen to Our Older Brothers and Sisters

Being more closely united to Christ, those who dwell in heaven
fix the whole Church more firmly in holiness. ...
[T]hey do not cease to intercede with the Father for us, as
they proffer the merits which they acquired on earth through
the one mediator between God and men, Christ Jesus. ... So
by their fraternal concern is our weakness greatly helped.

CCC 956

Catholic parents are never alone. The saints always have our backs. We just have to call on them!

We should start by always seeking the Holy Family's help. In our home, we ask for the Blessed Mother's intercession for everything from seeing that we don't burn dinner, to helping us correct our children as gently as she corrected Jesus when he was getting underfoot (being sinless doesn't mean he was never in the way)! Likewise, we regularly ask Saint

Joseph to coach us in being patient, loving, generous, faithful, and strong parents who put God's will before our own. The love the Holy Family shared and the example they set isn't just some abstract ideal; it's a model for all families.[1] The more we reflect on them and ask them for their prayers, the more we can become like them.

A Special Saint for Parents

Saint John Bosco is another really important saint for Catholic families. He wasn't a parent, but he was a great Christian teacher and the founder of a religious order (the Salesians) dedicated to helping and educating children. Many of the students Saint John Bosco taught were homeless or delinquent. At the time, people believed that children in general — and these kids in particular — were little better than animals who responded only to physical punishment and harsh correction. One day, the Blessed Mother visited Saint John Bosco in a vision. She told him that children should be corrected, "not with blows, but with sweetness and charity."

Deeply moved by this vision, Saint John developed a system of discipline he called The Preventive System, in contrast to what he considered to be the heavy-handed "repressive system" of his day. He taught his followers that even the most willful, defiant children would offer their heartfelt obedience if they were treated with love and respect. He argued that Christian discipline shouldn't just be about getting kids to behave. It had to be about evangelizing children in the way of love and virtue. He said that his method "consists in making known the rules and regulations ... and then supervising in such a way that the students are always under the vigilant eye of the [caregivers], who like loving fathers will converse with them, act as guides in every event, counsel them and lovingly correct them, which is as much as to say, will put the [children] into a situation where they cannot do wrong."

Saint John Bosco never wanted to lead his students into temptation. He preferred to focus on teaching children what to do and then supporting their success, as opposed to ignoring children until they misbehaved and then punishing them after the fact. The preventive system forms children's characters through "reason, religion, and loving-kindness." Regarding the harsh punishments popular in the day, the saint famously said, "To strike [a child] in any way ... should be absolutely avoided, because … they greatly irritate the young, and they degrade the educator." In this, he echoed the sentiments of another great saint, Saint John Chrysostom, a Doctor of the Church (an official Church title given to saints whose teachings are especially important to understanding our faith) who said, "Accustom (your child) not to be trained by the rod; for if he feel it … he will learn to despise it. And when he has learnt to despise it, he has reduced thy system to naught."

We're unaware of any other saint besides John Bosco who has offered the Church such a comprehensive system of child-rearing, but other holy men and women, such as the Boys and Girls Town founder, Servant of God Father Ed Flanagan, and famed Catholic educators Maria Montessori and Sofia Cavalletti (who developed the Catechesis of the Good Shepherd, an approach to religious education based on Montessori's methods), also advocated similar loving-guidance approaches to discipline. All of these great Catholic men and women recognized that the best way to help children be their best was to uphold remarkably high standards but support their success via the gentlest means. We'll discuss many gentle, remarkably effective discipline techniques in future chapters. But for now, it's enough to understand our basis for asserting that a loving-guidance approach to discipline is more consistent with our Catholic faith.

Of course, all of the saints have something to teach us. Just like you might message your best friend for a little parenting sympathy and support, don't forget to ask for the saints' intercession — especially on those tough days when you feel like you don't have an ounce of strength left or a friend in the world. Asking for the saints' help is more than a pious practice. It's a lifesaver!

Prayer

Lord Jesus Christ, help me to correct your children like your Mother instructed Saint John Bosco to correct the children you placed in his care: "with sweetness and charity." Help me to remember how patient and merciful you are with me when I fail you. Give me the grace to extend similar mercy to my children when they let me down and frustrate me. Let me always choose methods of correction that are rooted not in fear, but love, and help me model the way of love and virtue in my relationship with them. Let me show my children that following your way is not just the right thing to do, but the path to a happy, healthy, holy life.

Holy Family and Saint John Bosco, pray for us! Amen.

Discussion Questions

How do you ask for the saints' intercession to help you be a godly, effective parent?

How do Saint John Bosco's teachings challenge or support your ideas about good faithful discipline?

In what situations do you most need God's grace to correct more gently or charitably? What would you do differently? What saint will you ask for help to follow through with this resolution?

CHAPTER 6

The Sixth Difference: Parenting Is a Ministry

So great and splendid is the educational ministry of Christian parents that Saint Thomas has no hesitation in comparing it with the ministry of priests: "Some only propagate and guard spiritual life by a spiritual ministry: this is the role of the sacrament of Orders; others do this for both corporal and spiritual life, and this is brought about by the sacrament of marriage, by which a man and a woman join in order to beget offspring and bring them up to worship God."

Pope Saint John Paul II, *Familiaris Consortio*, 38

By now you know that family life is not an obstacle to living a holy life nor to doing important work for God's kingdom. But as we bring part one to a close, we wanted to emphasize that *Catholic parenting and family life are truly ministries* in the eyes of the Church.

How you parent really matters, not just to your kids but to your Church, your community, and yes, to God. Your work as a Catholic parent is an actual ministry. As we mentioned in chapter four, "ministry" isn't just the "churchy stuff we do at church." It is any activity that communicates God's love to another person.

The Church teaches that family life is the most important ministry work moms and dads can do! That's another sense of the phrase "domestic church." Being a lector, or leading the music at Mass, or even volunteering for a charity are all wonderful ministries, but God would have an easier time finding someone else to do any of those things than he would finding someone else to lead your children to him. Catholic parents are meant to build the kingdom of God primarily by dedicating themselves 100 percent to creating joyful, loving, godly homes and raising joyful, loving, godly kids. Think of how different the world would be if every Catholic family took this mission seriously.

Many Catholic parents feel selfish thinking of parenting as "ministry." They often tell us it feels like trying to get credit for something they'd have to do anyway. Frankly, this view reveals the unintentional, "do whatever works for you" approach most people have toward parenting. What makes parenting a ministry isn't the fact that you do it. It is the way you do it. No, parenting isn't a ministry if you roll out of bed and mindlessly trudge through the day, day after day. But if you do your best — in the face of your very real limitations and struggles — to fill every interaction with your kids with Christ's love, you will change the world.

There is an entire science called *ethnopediatrics* that studies the effect parenting styles have on the culture at large. We tend to think that culture is mainly about language, the arts, religion, etc. But long before people engage in any of these cultural activities, *they are parented.*

In her book, *Our Babies, Ourselves,* Cornell anthropologist Meredith Small argues that a culture's approach to parenting shapes that society's use of language, its approach to the arts, the values and worldview it promotes, and even its attitude toward spirituality, faith, and values. As Saint John Paul famously said, "As the family goes, so goes the nation and so goes the whole world in which we live." Small argues that the parenting methods advocated by a particular culture do more to impact its worldview than almost any other factor.

Of course, there's no guarantee that a particular parenting style will automatically produce children who are perfect models of a culture's values. But, Small argues, different cultures advocate different parenting practices because they've found, through centuries of trial and error, that certain parenting practices are consistently significantly more likely to promote certain values than other parenting practices.

Why is this important to Catholic parents? Because Catholics are called to evangelize the culture.[1] The Church challenges Christian families to build a "civilization of love," filling the world with children who are capable of exemplifying the self-giving love that comes from the very heart of God.

Most of us aren't going to create great works of art, or develop new languages, or come up with brilliant theological or philosophical insights, or even perform heroic acts that will be spoken of for generations. But every single Catholic family can choose to parent in a way that shows what God's generous, joyful love looks like in practice. The world desperately needs godly, loving, generous people. As Catholic parents, you are in the best position to give the world exactly what it needs. The way you parent your children today will affect the world for generations to come. The example you set will become the example your children and grandchildren will most likely default to in parenting their own children.

As we already mentioned, "self-giving" is the virtue that most clearly defines the "civilization of love" that Catholic parents are called to build. When Catholic parents follow Christ's example of self-giving love in our relationship with our kids, we not only grow in personal holiness, but we also celebrate the power of the "ministry of family life" to transform the world through our example.

If you would like to learn more about how to relate to parenting as a ministry, check out our books, *Discovering God Together: The Catholic Guide to Raising Faithful Kids* and *The Corporal Works of Mommy (and Daddy Too!)*. We would also like to invite you to sign up for The Catholic HŌM, a parenting program available for parishes or online at Catholichom.org. Likewise, we hope you'll take advantage of the online courses we developed for the Ministry of Parenting track through the Catechetical Institute at Franciscan University at https://www.catechetics.com.

Prayer

Lord, help me to always remember that parenting is my primary ministry; that the way I parent is the most important way you show your children how much you love them. Help me build a strong domestic church. Show me how to make our family a light to the world that draws others to you — not just in spite of our weaknesses, struggles, and challenges, but in the way we respond to our weaknesses, struggles, and challenges. Make us a family after your own heart.

Holy Family, pray for us. Amen.

Questions for Discussion

What does it mean to you to think of parenting as a ministry? How does it change the way you view your role?

What messages does your relationship with your children communicate about the way God loves them? What might you want to change in your relationship with your children so that you could more effectively communicate God's love to them?

What message do you think your family life sends to others about the ability of your Catholic faith to create warm, loving, joyful, generous people? What small changes might you want to make to become an even better witness to the power of God's love in your home? What support might you need to make those changes?

• • •

Conclusion to Part One

So, there you have it! Catholic families are called to be different from other families in the way they relate to one another and the world because:

- God is our co-parent, and we prayerfully invite him into every part of our day.
- Our families are icons of the Trinity. The love we share in our homes isn't based on any human model — including our families of origin — but rather the self-giving, familial love we find at the heart of God.
- Our families are domestic churches that model ourselves after God's family, the Church.
- We're on a mission to create communion, serve life, bless others, and share Christ in all we do.
- We turn to the saints for inspiration, guidance, and prayer support.
- We recognize that parenting is a ministry that's meant to give the world what it needs most: the next generation of loving, godly people.

The Church will never say, "Here are the parenting techniques you must use to be a great Catholic parent," but, as you see, she does present very clear ideas about how Catholic families are called to live and the mission Catholic parents are called to serve. Likewise, science offers important insights about the kinds of parenting practices that can help Catholic parents live out this vision in practical, meaningful, and manageable ways. The most "Catholic" method of parenting is the one that draws its recommendations from Saint Thomas Aquinas' "two books" of revelation: faith and science.

Having explored the vision, let's look more closely at what all this looks like in practice and give you the tools you need to build your dynamic domestic church and raise your kids to be loving, godly disciples of Christ.

PART TWO
Discipleship Parenting

Catholic parents aren't just called to raise kids. We're called to raise passionate followers of Jesus Christ — young men and women who know how to love God with all their hearts, minds, souls, and strength and their neighbors as themselves (see Mt 22:37–39). More than parenting children, Catholic parents are called to *disciple* them.

Over the years, we have searched for an appropriate name for the kind of parenting style we advocate. Recently, a friend and colleague of ours, author Kim Cameron-Smith, coined the term "Discipleship Parenting." We're happy to recommend her excellent book, *Discipleship Parenting: Planting the Seeds of Faith*. With her gracious permission, we also use this term to describe our approach.

Discipleship Parenting is the process by which the child's heart is turned (and re-turned) toward his parents at every stage of development so that Mom and Dad can ultimately bring their child's heart to God. Through this process, parents also learn to hear God's voice speaking to them through their children, inviting them to grow and heal as well. Discipleship is a relationship where both the follower and the mentor help *each other* grow closer to God through the process of accompaniment.

In the following chapters, you'll discover what science can teach us about the most effective ways to train your children in the way they should go so that even when they are adults, they will not depart from it (see Prv 22:6).

CHAPTER 7

Having a Ball: Discipleship and Attachment

Be fertile and multiply.

Genesis 1:28

Go, therefore, and make disciples ...

Matthew 28:19

Let the children come to me ... for the kingdom of heaven belongs to such as these.

Matthew 19:14

Discipleship Parenting is a lot like teaching your kids to play catch. When you play the game of catch, you watch how the other person throws the ball, and you try to throw it back in ways that they can catch it. Sometimes, you might mix things up. Maybe you throw it faster or slower. Maybe you throw a curveball once in a while. It can be fun to mix it up. But the goal isn't to intentionally make the other person miss. In a good game of catch, you try to help each other get better at sending the ball back and forth in a variety of variations, and you try to keep the ball in play no matter how it's thrown to you.

In a similar way, Discipleship Parents work to maintain strong, supportive back-and-forth interactions with their kids so they can maintain good communication and rapport (both verbally and nonverbally). In this way, the relationship itself becomes the primary way Discipleship Parents share the Faith with their kids and lead them closer to God. Discipling anyone in the Faith — especially kids — isn't as much about telling as it is about *relating* (or, as Pope Francis puts it, "accompanying").

As with playing catch, most of this back and forth between parents and kids isn't verbal. In fact, more than 90 percent of communication is nonverbal. That's why Discipleship Parenting ideally starts in infancy. Babies and toddlers can't learn faith facts, but they can learn how much they're worth in God's eyes when their parents take time to gaze at them, comfort them, and meet their needs as generously as they're able. These pre-verbal faith lessons actually become ingrained in our neurology and muscle memory. They become the physiological foundation of our moral, spiritual, and emotional well-being.

Through the back-and-forth process of consistent, supportive responding and relating, the child communicates his or her needs to the parent, and the parent responds promptly, generously, and consistently to the child. This helps the child learn to meet his needs in a godly, efficient, respectful manner. Over time, by playing this relational "game of catch" around all the issues that develop the child's character, faith, and morals, the child learns that there is nothing they can throw at Mom or Dad that they can't handle. Parents might drop the ball once in a while, but never on purpose, and they always pick it back up again. Parents who cultivate this kind of relationship with their kids are much more likely to raise children who are happy to "catch" all the lessons Mom and Dad "throw" to them.[1]

Yer-r-r-r OUT!
But let's change up the game. Imagine playing catch with someone who was so distracted that they only threw the ball back every tenth time? Or what if every time they missed the ball, they made you chase it and blamed you for throwing the ball incorrectly? Or what if every time they

threw the ball they intentionally tried to *make* you miss it, and then criticized you for not having your head in the game? Even if these terrible teammates regularly took you to baseball games and read you books about great baseball players, would you know how to play the game? Would you want to? More likely, you'd be relieved when you finally got to leave the team and give it all up so you wouldn't have to feel so frustrated all the time.

All of these latter examples are ways that parents undermine their ability to disciple their children. The more we fail to respond to our children's needs, blame our kids for the breakdowns in our relationships with them, criticize and lecture them instead of actively helping them succeed, or use heavy-handed punitive parenting techniques that shame our kids instead of helping them learn from their mistakes, the more our children eventually get tired of playing ball with us. They find other people to play catch with or choose to play a different game (i.e., religion/values system) altogether.

As an illustration of this, there is a reason that most "nones" (i.e., adults who claim no faith) say that they lost their faith by age thirteen.[2] It has less to do with their religious formation than with the fact that their parents' faith failed to make a positive difference in the quality of their home life.[3] The fact that the parents of most "nones" didn't notice their children had lost their faith until six years later, when the kids finally stopped going to church as young adults, highlights the poor quality of relationships in many Christian households.

Whose Team Are You On?

Catholic parents often complain about how hard it is to compete with society or the culture or the media or peer influence. These things certainly play a role in shaping our kids, but research consistently shows that the stronger the parent-child bond is, the healthier a child's relationship will be with peers, media, and society as well.[4] By mastering the game of relationship "catch," Discipleship Parents can gently remind their children that, regardless of other influences, they belong to Mom, Dad, *and* God's team *first*.

At every age and stage of your child's development, from infancy through young adulthood (and beyond), Discipleship Parenting is about keeping up the positive, back-and-forth interplay that enables you to capture and keep your children's hearts so that you can train them in the ways of the Lord (see Prv 22:6). To this end, Discipleship Parenting is entirely dependent upon your ability to build strong attachment with your child.

You may or may not be familiar with the term "attachment parenting." If you are, that's not exactly what we're talking about here. Attachment parenting practices (e.g., babywearing, sleep-sharing, extended nursing, etc.) are certainly intended to promote healthy attachment, but these techniques aren't the same thing as attachment. In fact, it's possible to use attachment parenting practices in a way that can actually lead to a poorly attached child. More on that later.

Incline Your Heart to Me ...

Attachment is best understood as your children's gut-level conviction (far beyond a merely intellectual appreciation) that you are the primary person to whom they can confidently and consistently turn for help in meeting their needs and living their best life. Attachment doesn't refer to how close you feel to your child. It refers to how close your child feels to you. Attachment is the measure of how confident your child is that, whenever or however they throw the ball to you (i.e., communicate needs or express concerns), you will be able to catch it and throw it back well (i.e., help them meet those needs in godly, efficient, satisfying ways).

Attachment doesn't just relate to parent-child relationships, but also to friendships and romantic relationships as well. You know you are strongly attached to someone if you have a desire to be near them and accept their influence. You might say that you are strongly attached to someone if — more often than not — your first response to any situation is, "Even when I feel confident handling something myself, I enjoy sharing my experiences with so-and-so and seeking their help, support, and company." By contrast, you may be less attached to someone if you feel nervous about approaching them with your needs, worry about whether you can really count on them, or if it doesn't occur to you to approach them with your needs at all.

You've Got (Attachment) Style

Regardless of the strength of your attachment to a particular person, your general attachment style refers to the unconscious attitude you have toward all relationships. Broadly speaking, a person may have a *secure* or *insecure* attachment style.

If you have a secure attachment style, you expect to be treated well and you work hard to treat others well. You surround yourself with emotionally healthy, respectful, capable people who are good at giving and asking for support. By contrast, the more insecurely attached you are, the more you tend to surround yourself with people who take advantage of you and are dismissive of your needs. In the extreme, the most insecurely attached people try to avoid needing or being needed by others at all.

The good news is that everyone can develop secure attachment. God created an entire part of our brain to support it. Researchers refer to the structures of the brain that support healthy attachment as the *social brain*. The neurological hardware of the social brain comes preinstalled at birth, but the software has to be uploaded — mainly by parents — throughout childhood. If Mom and Dad don't do their job, people can learn to have healthier relationship styles later in life through a process called *earned secure attachment*. It's just harder to do it that way.

Contrary to popular opinion, it isn't that certain personalities just "can't do" secure attachment or "can't relate" to it. Our attachment style has everything to do with both how we were raised and how intentional we are in adulthood about creating healthy, intimate relationships.

A host of studies going back to the late 1940s show that children develop secure attachment when parents respond promptly, generously, and consistently to their child's physical, emotional, relational, and spiritual needs. This prompt, generous, and consistent attention results in the child naturally turning toward the parents — physically, emotionally, and spiritually. The securely attached child views Mom and Dad as the primary sources for acquiring the nurturance and guidance he or she needs to flourish in life.[5]

This "turning toward" love represented by secure attachment is the basis for an authentic domestic church-based spirituality. As Saint John Paul wrote in *Evangelium Vitae* ("The Gospel of Life"), "The celebration which gives meaning to every other form of prayer and worship is found in the family's actual daily life together, if it is a life of love and self-giving."[6] Building on this theme, theologian Philip Mamalaikis wrote, "Families are not church only when they read scriptures, pray, study the faith, or help the needy. They are church in their (turning toward) love."[7]

This is the love we discussed at length in Part One: the love that comes from the very heart of God and enables families to be icons of the Trinity and dynamic domestic churches. But what does it take to create the kind of relationship with your kids that makes them not just want to be your children but also your disciples?

The Evolution of Attachment

Attachment is a continuous process that must be fostered from infancy through young adulthood. It can be helped or hindered by how well parents deal with the needs and challenges a child expresses, not just in infancy, but at each stage of development.

In the infant and toddler years, parents encourage secure attachment by responding promptly, generously, and consistently to their infant's and toddler's cries, and keeping their babies as physically close to their body as they reasonably can throughout the day and night.

Attachment certainly yields profound emotional benefits, but it begins as a physical/biological relationship. In infancy and toddlerhood, the parent creates a discipleship relationship with the child's body, helping the child establish the physiological and neurological foundations necessary for self-mastery, self-control, and empathy. The parent's body literally teaches the child's body how to re-regulate itself when it experiences stress and frustration — which, for little ones, is pretty often!

Babies are born too early. That's to say, they're born before their brains are fully developed. Without the parent's help, the infant and toddler's body struggles to regulate itself in response to emotional ups and downs and stressful events. Secure attachment facilitates healthy brain development by enabling parents to "download" their own healthy and stable heart rate, breathing rate, and body temperature into the child's body. Ultimately, the more securely attached you are, the easier it is for your brain to manage stress, have a healthy emotional life, and fully participate in healthy relationships.

Again, attachment has to be nurtured throughout the child's life. In early childhood (ages three to six), parents foster attachment by taking time to teach their children the stories, rules, habits, and structures (i.e., routines and rituals) that facilitate a healthy way of life.

In middle childhood (ages six to ten), the parents foster strong attachment by helping their children manage school and peer challenges, discover their unique gifts and talents, and learn to use those gifts in positive ways. Through all this, the child learns how to be a functional, effective person.

In pre-adolescence and adolescence (ages eleven to nineteen), parents maintain strong attachment by helping their kids have meaningful relationships with peers and discover ways to make a positive difference in the world.

As the child matures, attachment-building practices become less physical and more psychological, emotional, relational, and spiritual. When parents maintain strong attachment with their child over the years, it sends the message, "You can always turn to me — first and foremost — to get what you need to lead a healthy, godly, fulfilling life." Of course, most parents say this, but fewer children actually *feel* it's true. The strength of the attachment the child feels predicts how likely it is that the child will open up when the parent invites him to do so.

You might be surprised to read that parents need to foster secure attachment throughout childhood and even into adulthood. Attachment doesn't just matter to babies. It's a continuum. A child becomes an adult with a secure attachment style because the attachment experiences he had throughout his childhood and adolescence build on each other. Parents who "do attachment parenting" (especially grudgingly) with their infant and toddler but go on to "parent like everyone else" as soon as they can justify it to themselves (or whomever they were doing it for) actually undermine their efforts to create secure attachment.

Attachment parenting in general, and Discipleship Parenting in particular, isn't a series of techniques you employ with your child. It's an invitation to create a different kind of relationship with your child — a more intimate, interactive, and intentional relationship. Healthy consistency of caregiving (as opposed to either benign neglect or scrupulous perfectionism) combined with generous affection, a real willingness to listen, and gentle discipline throughout the various ages and stages of childhood are the keys to fostering the secure attachment that stands at the heart of a strong Discipleship Parenting relationship.

Attachment on My Mind

As we've already suggested, attachment is more than a psychological or spiritual phenomenon. It carves itself into your child's brain. Research using functional imaging technology (*f*MRI, *f*PET) shows that consistent, healthy parental-attachment behaviors literally stimulate growth in the child's social brain, the neurological seat of relational, emotional, and moral reasoning.[8] Other studies illustrate that poor parental attachment behaviors inhibit the development of the child's social brain, which, in turn, diminishes the child's capacity for intimacy, empathy, pro-social behavior, and healthy moral reasoning.

Daniel Siegel (2012) is a distinguished fellow of the American Psychiatric Association and world-renowned expert on parenting style's impact on brain development. He has a cool Catholic connection too. In 1999, Saint John Paul asked Siegel to address the Pontifical Council for the Family — and the Holy Father personally — on attachment and the "maternal gaze." Siegel asserts that secure attachment is responsible for eight essential components of good mental health (see Table 1).

Table 1: Secure Attachment Facilitates the Eight Components of Good Mental Health

1. Body Regulation	The ability to keep the body's systems (e.g., heart rate, respiration, body temperature) coordinated and balanced. This facilitates emotional health. *For example: A racing heart/respiration can precipitate anxiety. Feelings of exhaustion or under-stimulation can precipitate depression.*
2. Attuned Communication	The ability to pick up on nonverbal cues (facial expressions, tones of voice, posture) that indicate how other people are feeling/responding to you.

3. Emotional Balance	The ability to be emotionally stimulated enough to remain engaged without being flooded by feelings.
4. Response Flexibility	The ability to pause before acting on impulses and choose the best response to a situation. *People with ADHD, compulsive anger, addictions, and other impulse-control problems struggle with this skill.*
5. Fear Modulation	The ability to consciously turn down the volume on fearful feelings.
6. Insight	The ability to link my past, present, and future in a way that helps me make sense of my life and view myself in a compassionate manner.
7. Empathy	The ability to have insight (as defined above) into other people, to make sense of other people's lives, and view them with compassion.
8. Moral Reasoning	The ability to delay gratification, make healthy sacrifices for others, and act from the perspective of the greater good.

The more securely attached a person is, the more they're able to demonstrate the eight social brain-based skills that support good mental, relational, and spiritual health. By contrast, the more insecurely attached a person is, the more they will struggle to consistently exhibit some or all of the eight foundational mental health skills.

Feeling Insecure?

People who are insecurely attached fall into one of two basic categories: *anxious attachment* and *avoidant attachment*. The first type, anxious attachment, results when parents respond in a habitually delayed, reluctant, grudging, or inconsistent manner to their child's needs. Parents who adopt this attitude often worry about spoiling their children with "too much" affection. These parents tend to give their children the message — explicitly or implicitly — that if they want love or approval, they'll need to get better grades, do more chores, etc., to prove themselves. Such parents often point to the fact that their kids are high performers as "proof" that their approach is working. Unfortunately, these parents tend to be blind to the cost of this approach to "success." Anxiously attached kids can grow up to be remarkably accomplished. They just never feel good about anything they do.

Returning to our analogy of discipleship as playing catch with our kids, parents who raise anxiously attached kids are the parents who are either so busy lecturing their children about how to throw the ball properly that they never actually play the game (i.e., have a real relationship) or they're too distracted to consistently catch the balls the child throws to them — but then say it's the child's fault. This child comes to believe that the game (i.e., relationship) doesn't go well because there's something wrong with *them*. If they only could try hard enough, they could finally make the game work the way it's supposed to.

Anxiously attached people are at high risk for scrupulosity/neurotic guilt, codependency, fears of abandonment, struggles with basic trust, poor self-care, anxiety disorders, substance abuse (particularly opioids), and the inappropriate use of affection/sex as a strategy to keep a romantic partner. As adults, they tend to attach themselves to people who can't love them and then blame themselves for being unable to get their needs met.

Are You Avoiding Me?

The second type of insecure attachment, avoidant attachment, results from parents' miserly responses to their child's emotional and relational needs. Parents of avoidantly attached children may not be — strictly speaking — abusive or neglectful, but they tend to be terminally disengaged, and are often punitive, unaffectionate, intolerant of emotional displays, and allergic to anything that looks too much like "neediness."

Using the "playing catch" analogy, parents who raise avoidantly attached kids tend to refuse to give their kid a ball (i.e., cultivate a relationship) in the first place, telling them that it builds character to figure out how to get their own ball. If the child does manage to find a ball to toss to Mom or Dad (i.e., attempts to initiate connection), the parents duck it — usually because they're doing something "more important." After a while, the child just stops playing (i.e., relating in emotionally meaningful ways) and learns to look down on people who want to play on a team (i.e., be in an emotionally meaningful relationship) as being needy and unable to occupy themselves.

Avoidantly attached people tend to be suspicious of relationships and exhibit an unhealthy sense of autonomy, poor insight, and impaired empathy. They tend to be workaholics who prefer chasing accomplishment over intimacy. They often display a selfish (e.g., consumer or power-based) approach to sex. They're also prone to anger control problems, substance abuse, and physical health complaints that are primarily caused by their inability to appropriately express needs and emotions.

God Attachment
Catholic parents have extra cause to be concerned about their child's attachment style. Research shows that a person's human attachment style usually corresponds very closely to their *God attachment style.*

Anxious God attachment leads people to view God as a punishing parent. Anxiously God attached Christians tend to feel that they're always at risk for wearing out God's love or trying his patience. They feel compelled to jump through hoops to try to win God's love.

By contrast, *avoidant God attachment* makes people either highly resistant to any relationship with God or relegates them to one that's rooted almost entirely in duty and rules over intimacy.[9]

In sum, a person's attachment style represents their unconscious, neurologically based inclination to turn toward or away from others and God. Without secure attachment, an individual's potential for achieving personal integration, healthy, emotionally deep, and rewarding human relationships, and an honest, intimate relationship with God is significantly compromised.

What About Me?
Some readers can get a little nervous at this point. Fear not. The good

news is that even if you have an anxious or avoidant attachment style, it's possible to develop "earned" secure attachment. This is done by working hard to have healthy adult relationships and committing to an ongoing plan for personal/emotional/spiritual growth as adults. Again, using the playing catch analogy, even if you were taught all the wrong ways to throw, or even if you learned that playing catch was stupid, finding a person who could serve as a loving, supportive, patient coach would go a long way toward helping you learn to play the game properly (i.e., have healthy back-and-forth relationships).

If you have an anxious or avoidant attachment style, working to securely attach your own child can also be a very healing process. This is especially true if you make sure to get the support you need (including, when necessary, counseling) to deal with the sometimes surprising sense of resentment or anger that can emerge as you struggle with the feeling that *No one ever gave* me *this kind of love or attention. How* dare *my child demand so much from me!* Getting the support you need to move past this painful resistance is both worthwhile and deeply healing. We will discuss this process in greater detail in chapter nine.

The most important takeaway in this chapter is that fostering strong attachment with your children through every age and stage is the key to creating a discipleship relationship with your child. Strong attachment gives your child confidence that you can shepherd them toward a healthy, fulfilling, godly life. It makes your child resistant to unhealthy peer, media, and cultural influence. It makes your child want to listen to you, learn from you, and follow your lead without you having to resort to heavy-handed punishments and threats to get their attention.

Having explored the power of attachment to form healthy hearts and minds, the next chapter will look at how to use this power to build a House of Discipleship.

Prayer

Lord, help me to be your face of love to my children. Help me to attach my children's hearts to yours through the loving relationship I build with them day by day. Help me earn my children's trust at every stage and let them see me as their primary model for living a healthy, godly life. Make me a good disciple so I can raise my children to be even better disciples and follow you all the days of their lives.

Holy Family, pray for us! Amen.

Discussion Questions

Do you think you have more of a secure, anxious, or avoidant attachment style?

Regardless of your attachment style, you can always develop more secure attachments. How did the information in this chapter challenge your attitudes toward relationships in general and parenting in particular?

What attachment style do you think you have been fostering in your children? Regardless of your answer, what do you think you could do to foster a stronger attachment bond with your kids?

CHAPTER 8

Building a House of Discipleship

Parents have the first responsibility for the education of their children. They bear witness to this responsibility first by creating a home where tenderness, forgiveness, respect, fidelity, and disinterested service are the rule. The home is well suited for education in the virtues. This requires an apprenticeship in self-denial, sound judgment, and self-mastery — the preconditions of all true freedom.

CCC 2223

Every child needs secure attachment to thrive, but Discipleship Parenting takes the process of attachment one step further. Discipleship Parenting builds on strong attachment to accomplish two goals:

1. Give children a physical, bone-deep experience of the generous, extravagant love that comes from God's own heart.
2. Make children want to willingly turn to Mom and Dad to learn the lessons and skills they will need to live a truly loving, godly, fulfilling life in Christ.

We don't mean to suggest that other parents don't also want these things for their children. Of course they do. But there's a big difference between meaning to do something and actually doing it. Research consistently shows that a parent is only able to disciple their children into a healthy faith life and moral vision (i.e., one that's rooted in love rather than fear) to the degree that they are first able to foster at least some degree of secure attachment with their child. The opposite is also true. The more a child resists their parents' attempts to form their faith or moral life, the weaker the attachment tends to be between the child and the parent.

The House of Discipleship

Discipleship Parenting recognizes that raising up godly children is not primarily an intellectual exercise, but a relational one. At each stage of a child's development, Discipleship Parents use the strong attachment they foster with their children as the construction materials they need to build a warm, loving, grace-filled House of Discipleship.

As you can see in the House of Discipleship graphic, Discipleship Parents begin the process of raising godly, healthy children by helping their infants and toddlers learn how to *regulate their bodily reactions and impulses*, fostering the physical and neurological basis for trust, self-control, and empathy. These qualities become brain-based building blocks for faith and moral reasoning.[1]

Next, in early childhood, Discipleship Parents help their kids develop the *foundations of a Christian worldview* by establishing a loving environment in which the stories, rules, and structures that make up an orderly, peaceful life can be learned.

In middle childhood, Discipleship Parents *plant the seeds of their child's future vocation* by helping their child develop their unique gifts and talents. They also help their children learn to use their gifts to both make meaningful contributions to family life and have a positive impact on their peers.

Finally, in adolescence, Discipleship Parents show teens how their faith and moral vision can help them *develop healthy, meaningful, godly relationships and discover God's plan for their place in the world.*

At every stage of the discipleship process, the parent recognizes that this mentoring relationship isn't just a duty the child owes to them. It is

House of Discipleship

Stage Four: Relational Discipleship (Adolescence)

Teen turns toward parent to develop skills for having godly relationships and finding place in world.

Stage Three: Vocational Discipleship (Middle Childhood)

Child turns toward parent to discover and develop gifts in a way that helps him glorify God and make meaningful contributions to family and others.

Stage Two: Foundational Discipleship (Early Childhood)

Child turns toward parent to learn the stories, rules, and structures that lead to a love-filled, well-ordered life.

Stage One: Embodied Discipleship (Infancy and Toddlerhood)

Child turns toward parent to learn self-regulation and empathy through body-to-body communication.

mainly a connection that must be cultivated by the parent. Although we owe obedience to God, our heavenly Father doesn't wait for us to come to him. He runs to meet us on the road (see Lk 15:20). Discipleship Parents seek to follow the Father's example by not simply demanding or assuming a relationship with our children, but rather eagerly pursuing that relationship.

By lovingly investing our time in our children and cultivating an open-hearted attitude toward our children, Discipleship Parents send the message, "I am committed to helping you meet your (physical, psychosocial, relational) needs in a way that will satisfy you and keep you on a godly path." This is the message that will keep your child turning toward you even as his needs become more complicated and his social network expands.

We'll offer specific suggestions for ways parents can keep building a strong House of Discipleship in the chapters that explore each stage of childhood. For now, it's enough to know that not only is a discipleship relationship possible between parents and children at every age and stage, but also that this is exactly the kind of relationship the Church's theology of family intends parents to cultivate within their homes.

Attachment is the single most important tool you have in your toolbox. Everything else depends upon it. The effectiveness of *any* discipline approach (ours or anyone else's) is directly dependent upon the strength of attachment between parents and children. The weaker the attachment bond, the more children push back against their parents' guidance and the more parents are forced to rely on heavy-handed, punishment-based strategies to compel their children to listen to them. This latter approach is common enough — even in many Catholic households. Even so, this approach is completely inconsistent with our call to follow the example of the Good Shepherd as we patiently and gently lead our little sheep to the Father.

What It's NOT ...

Discipleship Parenting vs. Spoiling

As we wrap up this chapter, it's important to offer a few words of clarification. First, many people express the concern that responding promptly, generously, and consistently to their children will spoil them. This is an understandable concern, especially for Christian parents. Let's reflect on what spoiling actually means.

Popularly, people think "spoiling" is the same as being generous. Not only is this psychologically wrongheaded, it's directly contrary to how every Christian is called to live. Remember, the Church teaches that we become fully human by challenging ourselves to be more generous to others (see *Gaudium et Spes*). Likewise, we are called to follow God's example — and God is immeasurably generous. In fact, God is so generous, the psalmist tells us that he starts responding before our prayer leaves our mouths (Ps 139:4). Repeatedly throughout the Gospels, Christ generously gives more than people can possibly receive: more wine than is needed, more loaves than anyone knows what to do with, more fish than the nets can hold. The Christian God created an entire universe that most of us will never see, just in case we might one day want to explore it. The Christian God is ridiculously, insanely extravagant in his providence, love, mercy, and grace. As Christians, we're called to be similarly generous. Reflecting on our heavenly Father's example, we see that it's more than possible to be incredibly generous to others, including children, without spoiling them.

Children aren't spoiled because we are generous to them. They are spoiled when we are generous without requiring them to give back as much as they're capable of at each age and stage. This is exactly the model Christ uses. Jesus gives us his whole self freely — but heaven isn't free. It's only open to those who respond to Jesus' invitation and give themselves totally back to him. In a similar way, relationships between any two people — especially parents and children — only thrive when both people in that relationship are doing everything they can to give 100 percent to each other. Saint John Paul referred to this as "mutual self-donation." Mutual self-donation is the dynamic that exists between any group of people who consistently challenge themselves to promptly, generously, and consistently respond to one another's needs so that everyone in the relationship is able to flourish. This is the basis for the civilization of love Saint John Paul said it was every Christian's duty to create.

We don't flourish by being stingy. Misers don't live abundant lives. Neither do we prevent others from being spoiled and selfish by being stingy with them. In fact, deprivation is exactly what causes a selfish, grasping, self-protective attitude in children and adults.

Discipleship Parents strive to be heroically generous to their children, but they avoid spoiling their children by requiring them to give back to the family and to others as much as they're able as they grow and mature. In infancy and toddlerhood, children are completely incapable of taking care of themselves, much less giving back to their moms and dads in practical ways. In these early years, Discipleship Parents lay the neurological foundations of the "turning toward" relationship they want to have with their children.

In early childhood, children whose parents modeled this self-giving generosity naturally try to be generous and affectionate and to help out around the house in their way. Parents do well to encourage this "helpful" play — even when it's sometimes less than helpful. These early attempts to give back to Mom and Dad can be shaped into self-giving habits that allow the child to make real contributions to the household when they get a little older.

As the child matures into middle childhood, adolescence, and young adulthood, Discipleship Parents continue to respond as generously as they can to their children's needs while helping the child take on more responsibilities around the house and challenging the child to be as generous to his siblings, friends, and the community as Mom and Dad have tried to be to him. We'll talk more about what this generosity looks like in the future chapters on the ages and stages of childhood. For now, it's enough to know that being generous to our children doesn't mean giving them everything they want, the way they want it, and when. It simply means that you are committed to tuning in to your child, helping them identify the needs that drive their behavior, and accompanying them in the search for godly, fulfilling ways to meet those needs.

Discipleship Parenting vs. Helicopter and Rapunzel Parenting

Some well-meaning parents confuse attachment and discipleship with either helicopter parenting or what we will call "Rapunzel parenting." These latter approaches are very different from healthy Discipleship Parenting.

In addition to providing skills and support, Discipleship Parents are invested in giving children the space they need to struggle and succeed in a nurturing environment. By contrast, helicopter parents tend to focus on telling their children what to do, but never giving them an opportunity to do it, much less the space they need to do it independently. Helicopter parenting is really an anti-discipleship relationship based in fear, not love. Helicopter parents are always around, but their presence fosters anxious attachment. They are so busy telling their child all the rules for throwing the ball (and all the things that could go wrong) that they never allow the child to actually play. That makes kids nervous when it's their turn at bat.

The same is true for what we call Rapunzel parenting. Again, certain well-meaning Catholic parents believe that if — like the witch in the story of Rapunzel — they can just keep their child away from all influences that could compete with their own authority as parents, they will succeed in raising godly children. As the Rapunzel story illustrates, however, the opposite is more often true. Like helicopter parenting, Rapunzel parenting is also an anti-discipleship, fear-based relationship. Returning to our playing catch metaphor, Rapunzel parents allow their child to watch classic sports TV shows with the promise that if the child is attentive enough, one day they will learn to be great catchers too. Unfortunately, this approach often results in a moralistic person who knows how everything "should" be, but can't actually cope with the messiness of real life.

In our professional experience, helicopter and Rapunzel parents are motivated by the fear that their child's mistakes will reflect poorly on them. Helicopter and Rapunzel parents are so overly concerned about being judged that they are afraid to put their children in situations where their lessons could be tested and honed. To be frank, the tendency for parents to treat parenting like a show that they put on for other parents is the biggest contributor to parental burnout and poor parenting outcomes. God did not give us children so we could prove ourselves to our peers. He gave us children so that we could show them how to love God with all their heart, mind, soul, and strength and love their neighbors as themselves. The sooner moms and dads reckon with that, the happier they and their children will be.

The alternative to either helicopter or Rapunzel parenting is not simply letting the child struggle it out for himself in the school of hard knocks. Rather, it is *discipling* the child into success just like Saint John Bosco taught. Discipleship Parents provide the skills, support, and space their kids need to learn self-mastery and success in an environment where it's safe to make and learn from mistakes. Finding this balance can be challenging. It looks a little different with every child. We will give you guideposts throughout this book to help you find your way.

As we conclude this chapter, we hope that you will see that, for the Catholic parent, raising children is about approaching child-rearing as a process of discipleship. Through this process, you are meant to cultivate a relationship with your child that helps him love God and others as he has first been loved — by you.

Prayer

Lord, please open my heart wide to my children. Let them find you looking out at them through my eyes and experience your love pouring out of my heart. Help me to draw them close to me at every age and stage so that I can ultimately lead them to you. Make me as generous to them as you are to me, and let my example inspire them to work for the good of our household and all the people you place in their path as they grow into godly adults. May the love that comes from your heart shine out through my family and draw all the world to you.

Holy Family, pray for us. Amen.

Questions for Reflection

How does the idea of Discipleship Parenting challenge your idea of what it means to be a Catholic parent?

In what ways did your parents practice at least some aspects of Discipleship Parenting? Were their efforts to get you to turn toward them and listen to them rooted in love or fear? How might your childhood have been different if your parents had used the ideas we describe in this chapter?

How do the ideas outlined in this chapter compare to your current relationship with/attitude toward your child(ren)? What might change if you were to begin using more of these ideas in your relationship with your child?

CHAPTER 9

The Healing Power of Discipleship Parenting

*By calling God "Father," the language of faith ... thus
draws on the human experience of parents, who are in
a way the first representatives of God for man. But this
experience also tells us that human parents are fallible and
can disfigure the face of fatherhood and motherhood.*

CCC 239

*By knowing how to acknowledge their own failings to their
children, parents will be better able to guide and correct them.*

CCC 2223

*I will give you a new heart, and a new spirit I will
put within you. I will remove the heart of stone
from your flesh and give you a heart of flesh.*

Ezekiel 36:26

We can't give what we don't have. Discipleship Parenting isn't only about attending to our children. It is also about understanding how God uses our parenthood to heal the wounds we all carry inside that make it difficult to receive the love our heavenly Father wants to give us.

The Struggle Is Real

As you try to apply the suggestions in this book, you may be surprised to find your own woundedness sometimes getting in the way. Maybe you feel stressed or anxious. Perhaps you feel cynical, irritated, or resentful. Maybe you feel tempted to parent in a scrupulous manner that leads to self-criticism and burnout. Maybe there's even a part of you that resists the idea of creating a truly intimate, discipleship bond with your child because it feels strange, forced, or somehow unnatural or even wrong. These feelings don't mean that there is something uniquely wrong with you. They just mean you're human. Even so, the more we give in to these reactions, the harder it is for us to experience parenting as the healing experience God wants it to be *for us*. The struggles you encounter as you attempt to practice Discipleship Parenting are not the result of some personality issue that you simply have to accept. They are evidence of a spiritual wound that God wants to heal.

Made for Love

We were all created for love. As God's children, we're destined to spend eternity in a loving, intimate communion with God and all the saints. Unfortunately, sin can make even the idea of this intimate, close communion seem foreign. That's why God wants us to spend our time on earth learning how to be as fully intimate as we can with the people who share our lives — especially our children. Remember what Jesus said: "Amen, I say to you, unless you turn and become like children, you will not enter the kingdom of heaven" (Mt 18:3).

The more we work to create this intimate connection — especially with our spouse and children — the more healed and fully human we become *and* the more we prepare ourselves to share in our heavenly destiny. Discipleship Parenting is ultimately a healing enterprise because it is an education in the kind of self-giving love that makes us whole and holy.

It's true that Discipleship Parenting may come more naturally to some parents than others, but it involves challenges for everyone. Learning to love ourselves and our children with the love that comes from God's heart is hard work! That said, any struggle or resistance we may encounter in establishing a securely attached, discipleship relationship with our children is not due to the way we "are." *It's due to the way we were hurt.* The struggles we experience in fostering a strong attachment/ discipleship relationship with our children are usually related to how much our own parents struggled to meet our emotional, relational, or spiritual needs growing up. Our heavenly Father wants to heal those wounds. He wants to meet those needs. The heart-to-heart connection Discipleship Parenting seeks to create between God, you, and your child allows the Lord's healing grace to fill the empty, dark spaces that are sometimes uncovered when we're trying to give our children the love God wants them to have. Remember God's promise, "I will give you a new heart, and a new spirit I will put within you. I will remove the heart of stone from your flesh and give you a heart of flesh" (Ez 36:26). God wants to fulfill this promise through the ministry of parenting in your domestic church.

The Parent Trap: Work vs. Toil

The world tells us that parenting is meant to be a thankless, exhausting, frustrating task. Many Catholic parents we have encountered seem to believe, at least implicitly, that parenting is only holy to the degree that it is hard and miserable. In light of these messages, it can be difficult to believe that parenting could be a source of anything except migraines.

We're not saying that parenting at any stage — especially in the infancy and toddler years — is easy. We also don't mean to suggest that if you feel tired, frustrated, resentful, or angry some days, and even several days at a time — that there is something wrong with you or your children. There isn't. Every parent experiences this from time to time. The fact that, once a child is born, most parents don't return to "normal" sleep schedules until their child is at least six years old can grate on the best of us.[1]

Yet, if every day feels like drudgery ... if you are in a constant battle with your kids ... if you feel perpetually drained, resentful, angry, or depleted … please know this is not what parenting — especially Discipleship Parenting — is meant to be. These feelings are clear signs that there is a need for deeper healing. Being a parent is hard work, but it's not meant to feel like a rock around your neck.

There is a difference between hard work and what is called "toil." The Book of Genesis reminds us that Adam and Eve were created to tend the Garden of Paradise. But before the Fall, when God, humankind, and creation existed in a harmonious relationship with one another, the work our first parents did was joyful. Adam and Even rejoiced in the ways God worked through them.

It was only after the Fall, when the relationship between God, humankind, and creation was shattered, that their work became toil. Toil is work that's mind-numbing, exhausting, and devoid of any sense of satisfaction or divine purpose. "Another day, another list of thankless, tiresome tasks." Does this sound like the way a lot of parents you know approach child-rearing? Maybe it even describes how you feel. If so, the good news is, there is a way out of this parenting trap.

The Way Out

Saint John Paul's Theology of the Body reminds us that for work to feel life-giving, it has to be relational. We have to do our work in a manner that keeps us connected to God, others, and our best selves.

Parenting is hard work, but it's only draining and soul-crushing toil if we give in to the temptation to see our children as burdens to be borne, projects to be managed, or tests we have to pass to prove our worth. As soon as we start thinking this way, the work of parenting becomes *toil*, and we start to burn out. The good news? When we focus on creating a discipleship *relationship* with our children, the hard work of parenting becomes a source of joy and healing. We experience God working in us, through us, and with us. Together with God's grace, we make our homes into graceful spaces filled with warmth and love — even when the going gets tough.

Here are some ways you can begin to unpack the healing power of Discipleship Parenting.

Release Your Priestly Power – Consecrate Every Moment

We unlock the healing power of Discipleship Parenting by consecrating every moment to Christ — good, bad, painful, joyful, and otherwise. That's more than a pious sentiment. It's a practical exercise for tapping into sacramental, healing grace. Here's how it works.

Through our baptism, we are initiated into the *common priesthood*. While it's the job of the *ministerial priesthood* to administer all the sacraments and, in particular, consecrate the bread and the wine into the Body and Blood of Christ, it's the job of the common priesthood (i.e., baptized laypeople) to consecrate the world to Christ. As we discussed in the very first chapter, Discipleship Parents need to invite God into every good, bad, and ugly moment of our domestic church life. When we do this, we consecrate these moments and make them a source of grace and healing. Through our running conversation with God, we practice listening to his voice speaking through each moment and telling us how to respond to that moment in a way that helps us become the whole, healed, godly, grace-filled people we're meant to be.

As common priests exercising the ministry of parenthood and witnessing to Christ's sacrificial love, we become a bridge between God and our kids.[2] God uses us as an instrument for filling our hearts, our homes, and our kids with this love.

The love we have for our children doesn't start with us. It actually comes from God and flows through us. You can tap into the healing power of this love as it flows through you. When you are holding your little one in your arms, close your eyes. Imagine that the love that you feel for your child is being poured into your heart by your heavenly Father. Look into your Father's eyes. See that the love you have for your child is just a fraction of the love God has for you — a tiny portion of the love God is pouring into your heart. Take a moment to revel in that love. Let it soak in. Offer up a brief prayer consecrating that moment to God. *Lord, I praise you for your abundant love. Fill up every part of me with your love and grace. Help me to never doubt my worth in your eyes, and help me be a perfect channel of your love for my child.*

In addition to this simple exercise, try to keep two questions in mind throughout your day. First, ask yourself, "How can I use this parenting moment to try to become a tiny bit more of the whole, healed, godly, grace-filled person God wants me to be?"

Second, when you struggle to be that whole, healed, godly, grace-filled person, ask yourself, "How can I let my limitations invite me to rely more on God's mercy and grace?" Remember, we need to be pleased to be works in progress. As God told Saint Paul, "My grace is sufficient for you, for power is made perfect in weakness" (2 Cor 12:9). Let God's grace fill the gaps you can't fill with your own energy.

Through these priestly acts of consecrating every moment to God and modeling Christ's sacrificial love the best you can, you release the healing power of your domestic church.

Release Your Prophetic Power – State Your Needs

In addition to your priestly mission, you were given a *prophetic mission* in baptism. We live out the prophetic mission of our baptism by showing others how to live the Faith in the real world (see CCC 785). One of the ways parents do this is by showing our kids — through our example — how to have a healthy relationship with our God-given needs.

Having a healthy relationship with our God-given needs doesn't mean either ignoring them or being bossy about them. It means meeting them in ways that give glory to God, respect the needs of others, and help us become the people we were created to be.

God made you. He also made your needs. Your needs tell the story of how God made you to not only survive, but to thrive. You must make sure your needs for nutrition, hygiene, respect, relationship, spiritual connection, and growth are being met. You can't do this all by yourself. You need help. Needing help doesn't mean you're an insufficient parent. It means you are functioning exactly the way God made you to function. Part of the reason God gave us needs is so that we would be inspired to turn to him and others for help. God expects us to bring our needs to one another. That's how we build the communities of love Saint John Paul talked about.

And here's something that often comes as a surprise to some readers. God wants you to *expect* that the people in your life will help you meet your needs every bit as much as you help them meet theirs. This is Saint John Paul's idea of "mutual self-donation" at work. It's mutual self-donation that makes relationships healthy, strong, and satisfying.

This is lost on a lot of parents, especially those with insecure attachment. Everyone has at least some difficulty telling other people their needs. It feels vulnerable and a little bit scary. But for people with an anxious attachment style, the very idea of having needs feels like a sin, never mind expecting others to help them meet those needs. Likewise, people with avoidant attachment are barely aware that they have needs, much less willing to admit them to anyone else.

Remember, Discipleship Parenting is about helping our children turn to us so that we can show them — by word and example — how to meet all their needs in godly, efficient ways. Teaching our kids to live abundant, godly lives is the prophetic ministry of parenthood. We can't teach kids godly ways to meet their needs if we aren't doing it ourselves.

As human beings, we suffer when we don't tell others what we need. Some Catholics have the mistaken impression that suffering automatically makes us holy. It doesn't. It's our *response* to suffering that makes us holy, and the only holy response to suffering is compassion. We must always do what we can to address the causes of suffering; to meet the need, address the concern, heal the wound. We must be compassionate to our own needs and the needs of others. As Jesus said, "Love your neighbor *as yourself.*" Discipleship Parents must learn to be compassionate toward the suffering of both their children *and themselves.*

If you feel guilty telling others what you need or getting others to take your needs seriously, these are serious problems that can undermine your mental health, the quality of your family life, and your ability to live your prophetic witness as a Discipleship Parent. We would like to gently encourage you to seek help in overcoming this struggle. Although there is more to this process than we can adequately address in these pages, books like *God Help Me! These People Are Driving Me Nuts* (which is about learning to be gracefully assertive) or *Unworried: A Life Without Anxiety* (which discusses how to fight anxiety by effectively meeting one's physical, emotional, relational, and spiritual needs) or *Then Comes Baby* (which explores how new parents can generously meet their child's needs while attending to their own needs as well) can be a good start. You may also learn more about the pastoral tele-counseling services we offer through CatholicCounselors.com if you would like more personal assistance.

Regardless of where you stand with this skill, finding godly ways to meet your needs while attending generously to the needs of others is an important way of exercising your prophetic mission and releasing the healing power of your domestic church.

Release Your Royal Power — Engage

Finally, in addition to the priestly and prophetic missions, we're also given a *royal mission* in baptism. We fulfill our royal mission by serving those around us with the love of Christ (see CCC 786). It isn't enough to serve to get things done. We must serve with godly love. Discipleship Parents exercise their royal mission not just by doing the tasks involved in keeping family life running smoothly (cleaning, cooking, maintaining, paying bills, etc.), but by trying to do them in a way that draws our kids closer to us and God. The following chart illustrates impoverished attitudes that undermine our royal mission in parenting versus healthy attitudes that support it.

Impoverished Attitude	Royal Attitude
When doing a task, I tend to push others out of the way because they always do it "wrong" and it's easier to do it myself.	When doing a task, I look for ways to include my kids so they can learn to help and serve.
I tend to rush around from task to task and struggle to find the time or energy to connect with my kids.	I try to pace myself when doing household tasks so that I can still talk/be present to my kids while I work.
I often feel put-upon or resentful about the things I have to do for my kids (and it probably shows).	Even when it's hard, I make an honest effort to do things for my kids in a way that communicates God's love for them.

I tend to feel like the things I do to take care of my family are more of a bother than a blessing.	I do my best to remember that the things I do to take care of my family mean a lot to them and make an important difference in their lives.
I'm frustrated that I never seem to get enough "me time" and, when I do, I hate coming back.	I take breaks when I need them, but I also get real joy from maintaining both my home and relationship with my kids.
I am much happier serving people outside my home than in it.	I enjoy my family and see them as my primary ministry. I only say "yes" to outside activities if they don't compete with my ability to be present to my family.

The point of this chart isn't to judge any parent who identifies more with the sentiments on the left rather than those on the right. It's simply to note that parents who work hard to cultivate the attitudes on the right tend to experience more life satisfaction in general, and get more joy out of parenting in particular. Sometimes, even the best parents have a difficult time maintaining these more positive attitudes. While it's important to do what you can to view your parenthood through this healthier lens, and sometimes it's necessary to fake it till you make it, this effort shouldn't feel perpetually forced or phony. If, despite your best attempts, you just can't bring yourself to break free of these more impoverished views toward family service, it might indicate that you are struggling with an attachment wound that requires professional help to heal. The attitudes on the left are quite common for people with anxious and avoidant attachment styles. The good news is, the impoverished views in the left column don't represent an immutable personality type. They aren't the way you are. They point to the ways you were hurt. Becoming aware of this opens up pathways for healing.

Ultimately, the more we lean into our royal mission as parents, the more we become resistant to burnout. *Burnout = Effort – Meaning.* The more we approach parenting as a series of thankless, never-ending tasks

that have nothing to do with relationship, the more we feel like cogs instead of people and the more burned-out we become.

Many burned-out parents try to recharge by getting away. Of course,
knowing when to take timely breaks is an important survival skill for every parent, especially if you use some of your time away to make a plan to
address the problems causing your stress in the first place. But research
on burnout suggests that leaning too heavily on time away can actually
increase our overall sense of dissatisfaction.[3] Although getting away can
feel good, you always have to go back again — usually to a bigger pile of
stuff to do.

A more effective strategy for beating burnout is recharging your
sense of meaning through *the practice of presence*. Essentially, that involves being more thoughtful and intentional about whatever you're doing. Making dinner? Think about *why* you're cooking — how each
bite of food makes your kids stronger and helps them grow into
the people they were created to be. Tidying up? Think about *why*
you're cleaning — how taking care of the things you've been given
is a way of saying "thank you" to God for his generosity and love.
Playing with your kids? Focus on really connecting with your children's smiles. Praise God for the creativity and joy in your children's
hearts. While you're at it, thank him for the reminder that it's OK to
be a little silly yourself.

Our book *The Corporal Works of Mommy (and Daddy Too!)* can
help you reengage your sense of meaningfulness by showing you how to
connect with the grace hiding just below the surface of all the things you
do all day. Embracing the royal mission of baptism heals our hearts by
helping us serve others out of a sense of genuine love and divine purpose.

Two Powerful Techniques

In addition to receiving the healing that comes from embracing the
priestly, prophetic, and royal dimensions of Discipleship Parenthood,
there are two powerful techniques that anyone can use to tap the healing
power of their domestic church: namely, the Four Questions Technique
and the Inside Out Exercise.

Four Questions Technique

Many of the struggles we face in creating strong attachments with our kids are rooted in unhealthy attitudes we learned in our families of origin. Healing these wounds requires us to become aware of the unconscious scripts that drive our actions so that we can intentionally redirect our emotional energy down healthier paths.

Parents occasionally respond to their kids in ways that they regret after the fact but feel powerless to change in the moment. The Four Question Technique can help you develop productive responses to your children's problem behaviors. When you feel disappointed in yourself for reacting poorly to your child, write out your reflections to the following four questions:

1. How did my mom and/or dad approach situations like this?
2. As a child, did their approach draw me closer to them or make me afraid of/close off to them?
3. Would I want my child to feel the same way toward me as I did toward my parent in this situation? If not, how would I like them to feel toward me?
4. How might I need to change my approach so that I can effectively address this problem, but still allow my child to feel the way I would have wanted toward my mom and/or dad?

Here are some examples of how parents have used this exercise to address the wounds that made it difficult for them to be their best selves with their kids:

Matt, a thirty-five-year-old father of three (ages five, two, and one), struggled with anger toward his children. Although he was never physically abusive, he would find himself screaming at his kids to the point that they started avoiding him. After one particularly ugly incident, his wife, Annette, demanded that he seek help. He continued to insist that, although he didn't like having to yell at his kids, they "made him do it" because of their constant disobedience and disrespect.

Matt related a time when he asked his five-year-old son to

pick up his toys. He said that his son ignored him, so he began yelling at the boy, lecturing him on the need to be respectful. His son started crying and ran to Annette. Matt was furious at what he considered his son's attempts to play his wife and him off of each other and Annette's willingness to be "manipulated" by their son.

We asked Matt, "How did your dad approach situations like this?" **(Question 1)**

Matt said, "Oh, man. He wouldn't have put up with the things my kids do."

"Really? What would he do?"

"If we didn't listen the first time, he would get up in our face and let us know that if we didn't get to it right then, that would be the end of us!" Matt chuckled with the memory. "The one or two times that we pushed it past that point, we got a spanking we wouldn't forget. You definitely did not cross my dad."

"It sounds like your dad was able to get you to do what he needed you to do. But did your dad's approach make you feel closer to him? Or did it make you afraid of him or want to close off to him?" **(Question 2)**

"I mean, I knew my dad loved me. He was a really good dad."

"I don't disagree that he loved you, and I know you've said how much you respect him even now. But did the way he handled these kinds of situations make you feel closer to him or did it make you afraid of him?"

"Well, we were close in lots of different ways, but I was definitely afraid then."

"Would you want your kids to feel the same way about you as you did your dad in those times?" **(Question 3)**

"You mean, do I want them to be afraid of me?"

"Yes."

"Well, I want them to respect me."

"Of course, but do you want them to be afraid of you the same way you felt afraid of your dad in those times?"

Matt hesitated a moment, and then shook his head. "No.

Like I said, I want my kids to respect me, but I would never want them to be afraid of me. Sometimes, when I walk into the room, I see the light go out of their eyes. Honestly, that kind of kills me."

"So, Matt, if we could find some ways to get your kids to respect you without you having to make them afraid of you, would that be OK?" **(Question 4)**

Matt sniffed as he blinked back a tear. "Oh, man. Um. I'm not sure why I'm tearing up right now. Something about this conversation's really hitting me hard. Um. Yeah. I'd like that."

We inherit a lot of scripts from our parents. When our kids push our buttons, we react. We remember that what our parents did "worked" in that it made us do what they wanted us to do. In the moment, that looks like the answer we've been searching for, and we latch on to it. Sometimes that's a good thing. Sometimes, not so much.

Going through the Four Questions Technique forces us to think a little bit deeper — to appreciate that our ends doesn't always justify our means. Every exchange we have with our kids makes them either open up or close off a little bit. Any single exchange doesn't make that much of a difference in the overall picture. But when an exchange becomes a pattern and the pattern defines the relationship, that's another thing altogether.

Leading Matt through the Four Questions Technique made him realize that he was losing their hearts. He connected with the fact that even though he always loved and respected his father, he never really felt close to his dad. He was determined to create a different kind of relationship with his own kids. That decision didn't just make him a better dad; it allowed him to begin healing the attachment wound at the heart of his anger.

Here's another example:

Marta was a new mom of a three-month-old girl, Grace. Marta shared that she wanted to nurse Grace, but every time she latched on, Marta felt deeply resentful. She said, "I'm ashamed to say it, but I hate sitting there and having this kid suck on me.

I know that sounds terrible, but it, like, feels … gross." Even though she knew "breast is best," she hated nursing and couldn't wait to stop. She was torn between her friends who kept telling her "some women just aren't cut out for nursing" and the part of her that hated the idea of "being a quitter." She forced herself to keep trying even though it made her feel "sick and totally stressed out." She felt she needed to keep it up for at least six months, but she was counting the days until she could stop. In session, we walked her through the four questions.

"How do you think your mom would have approached a situation like this?" **(Question 1)**

"That's a stupid question. She didn't nurse me. I was bottle-fed. She was proud of it. She always made fun of those moms who were into breastfeeding. Called them 'Nursing-Nazis.'"

"Right. I get that. But how did she approach situations **like** this? For instance, how was your mom when she had to just sit with you and be there for you?"

"Oh my God! Are you kidding? My mom never would just sit with us. She was a very 'Suck it up and get over it' kind of person. Yeah, no way would she have ever just sat there with me."

"Did the fact that your mom responded that way make you want to draw closer to her or make you afraid of her?" **(Question 2)**

Something about the question put Marta on the defensive. "I don't think it made me afraid of her."

"OK, but did the fact that she would never take the time to just sit with you and be with you make you want to draw closer to her or make you tend to stay away from her?"

"Well … no. She made it pretty clear she didn't think it was good to have too close a relationship with her. Her dad left them when she was little, and her mom fell apart after. She wanted us to learn to stand on our own."

"I can certainly see why she would have felt that way. So, you're saying that her approach didn't make it feel safe to draw closer to her?"

"I wouldn't say I didn't feel safe. I mean, it's not like she beat us or anything. But, no, I didn't feel like it would be worthwhile to try to get closer to her. She would have just thought I was being needy and she hated that."

"Do you think you would want Grace to feel like you didn't want her to be close to you? Or like you would think poorly of her for trying to be close to you?" **(Question 3)**

"That's ridiculous. She's a baby."

"Well, yes. But would you want her to feel like you didn't want her to be close to you or, even as a baby, that you would hate her trying to be close to you?"

Marta became very quiet. "I think that would be awful."

"Really? Why?"

"Because she's my baby and I love her. I … don't want her to feel anything except how much she means to me." Marta cleared her throat. "We named her 'Grace' because it took years for us to get pregnant. And then, one day, there she was. She's our gift from God."

"It sounds like you always want Grace to know what a blessing she really is to you."

"Yeah. I would. I don't ever want her to feel like anything else."

"So, how do you think that you could approach nursing Grace in a way that would help you address your discomfort, but still help her feel like she's a gift?" **(Question 4)**

"Wow. I'm … not sure. I guess, maybe try to nurse in a more comfortable space. Now that I think of it, I've always resisted getting a nursing chair or trying to create a comfortable place to do it. I just kind of latch her on and watch the clock waiting for her to stop. Maybe, if I stopped approaching the whole thing like it was a job and tried to make it a more pleasant experience for both of us that would be a start?"

Leading Marta through the four questions exercise helped her reconnect with the royal dignity of her motherhood. She decided to stop treating herself like a milking machine and start connecting with why she chose to nurse: to celebrate what a gift Grace is to her.

The Four Questions Technique isn't a one-off exercise. It's meant to be an ongoing conversation that we have with ourselves. Get a notebook. Identify a parenting situation that is frustrating you. Write your answers to the four questions. Integrate this exercise into your prayer life. When you identify how you wish you could have felt toward your parents, ask your heavenly Father to help fill that void. Bring him the wounded parts of yourself and ask him to fill those dark spaces with his love. Then, look for ways to communicate that love to your child. Let God heal you while you give your children the gift of an even more grace-filled childhood.

Inside Out Exercise
Another simple technique for dealing with the conflicted feelings that often accompany parenting is the Inside Out Exercise.

The Pixar film *Inside Out* tells the story of a little girl who struggles with adjusting to her family's move to a new home in a different part of the country. The film cleverly portrays the feelings of Joy, Sadness, Fear, and Disgust as distinct characters who live in her head. These four "people" have to learn to work together to help her navigate this difficult transition.

The film is actually based upon a psychological technique in which a person imagines their feeling as a separate person. For instance, you might describe your feeling of sadness as "a wrinkled, achy, tired old man." Or your anger as "a red-faced, tantrumming toddler." Or your resentment as "a sulky teenager dressed in black jeans and a T-shirt."

Researchers at the University of Texas conducted a study to examine the effectiveness of this technique. They had people describe an upsetting situation and rate their emotion on a scale of 1 to 10. Then they had the person describe their feeling as if it were a different person. What sort of person would the feeling look like? Once the participants anthropomorphized the feeling (i.e., described it as a person separate from them), the researchers asked the participants to rate the strength of their emotion once again. In every case, participants gave the feeling a significantly lower rating. They said they felt like the exercise helped them feel more detached from the negative feeling and claim more power over their emotions.[4]

For even greater effect, you can imagine having a conversation with this other "person." Specifically, imagine asking what that tired old man, tantrumming toddler, or sulky teen needs in order to feel loved and taken care of. You can even ask God to help you minister to this "person." Although some people can feel a little silly doing this at first, it has an almost universally powerful and positive effect. Here are some examples of the exercise at work.

Eric, thirty-five-year-old father of four children ages six and under

I used to get resentful of the time my wife gives to our kids. It frustrates me when we can't get a date or when she is too tired to be intimate. When I tried this exercise, the image that popped into my head was a sad 7-year-old standing there with a wilted flower waiting for the girl he had a crush on to pay attention to him. Praying about it, I felt sad for him, but God also helped me realize that unlike him, I already "got the girl." Doing this whenever those feelings come over me helps me remember that I'm not a lovesick little boy. My wife loves me, and having this family is something we took on together. Instead of just sitting there pouting and waiting for her to get the kids to bed so we could get some time together, thinking of my feelings this way helped me want to go and help her get them ready, read to the kids, and just be part of the whole nighttime routine. I enjoyed connecting around our bedtime routine. Plus it made her feel less stressed and more open to hanging out with me after.

Cynthia, twenty-nine-year-old mother of two — Noah (three) and a baby girl, Livy (six months)

I get so angry when my son either doesn't listen to me or comes barging in when I'm nursing Livy and trying to get her down for a nap. The anger just completely overtakes me. I end up screaming at Noah, which makes him cry, really gets Livy going, and sets me on edge the rest of the day. When I imagined that anger, I saw a mean, old, scary, green-skinned witch — you know, like the Wicked Witch in the *Wizard of Oz*? I call her "Witch-Lady." When I feel "her" coming out, I just close my eyes and imagine myself saying something like: "Seriously, Witch-Lady? Really? You running around trying to scare everybody into being quiet isn't helping anything. Just go hang out in your castle with your flying monkeys and stuff. I got this." I know it sounds dumb, but it actually gives me some perspective. I've actually been a lot more patient with the kids since I started doing this. Before, the anger just seemed so big, I couldn't fight it. Doing this made me feel like it was something I could handle. Even Witch-Lady is happier with me these days.

Ashley, thirty-two-year-old mother of three
Sometimes I feel really resentful toward the kids, especially if I'm tired or haven't had a chance to take care of myself for a few days. It gets to the point where every little thing gets on my nerves. I start snapping at the kids, barking at my husband, and just being a real joy to be around. When I close my eyes and imagine this feeling, I see a little girl, maybe two and a half or three. She's really tired. She's rubbing her eyes and stumbling around, walking into things and just ready to burst into tears at any moment. She just really needs a nap and a healthy snack. You know what I mean? I call her my "Tired Toddler."

Anyway, I used to beat up on myself for feeling resentful toward my kids. Like, "what kind of a horrible mom does that make me?" and stuff. Now, when my Tired Toddler comes out, I ask the Blessed Mother to help me take care of this little girl; to remember that she is precious in Jesus' eyes, just like my children are precious to me. It's really helped me see that that feeling of resentment is just a signal that "she" needs someone to take care of her a little bit. I make a point of imagining her sitting in "Mommy Mary's" lap. Then I tell the "little girl" that her needs are important too. Then I either make a plan to take better care of myself that day or, if I can't figure out how, I try to sit down with my husband and let him know what I'm going through so we can figure it out together. Doing this has made such a difference. I can't even tell you.

These techniques aren't meant to be a cure-all. If your strong, negative feelings are consistently undermining your efforts to be the parent or person you want to be, it would be good to seek professional assistance to get some new tools. But for the typical, day-to-day resentment, anger, self-doubt, sadness, and irritability all parents occasionally face, this exercise can be a game-changer.

Conclusion

Parenting can be tremendously difficult work. Besides the fact that taking care of little children can be physically and emotionally taxing, parenting also tends to bring up our own childhood wounds and the unresolved issues we have with our families of origin. As Christians, we don't have to fear this reality. Instead, we should embrace it as the healing opportunity it's meant to be. God wants to break through all the noise and busyness of our everyday lives to remind us that even while we work hard to give as much love as we can to our children, God wants to give all of that love and more to the hurting parts of our hearts. After all, we are all his children, first and foremost.

Recommended Resources for Additional Healing

Then Comes Baby: The Catholic Guide to Surviving and Thriving in the First Three Years of Parenthood (Dr. Greg and Lisa Popcak, Ave Maria Press)
Explores the challenges of the first three years of parenthood in detail. In addition to an in-depth look at all the questions Catholic parents have about creating strong attachment with infants and toddlers, we look at how parents can be sure to take care of themselves and their marriage and find balance in all the various needs that have to be attended to, so moms and dads can not merely survive, but thrive, in the early years of parenthood.

Parenting from the Inside Out: How a Deeper Self-Understanding Can Help You Raise Children Who Thrive (Daniel Siegel and Mary Hartzell, Tarcher-Perigee)
Helps parents identify and address the emotional baggage that can steal the joy from parenting at every age and stage. A must-read for every par-

ent, Siegel and Hartzell's book will be especially helpful to parents whose childhoods were less than ideal.

Homecoming: Reclaiming and Healing Your Inner Child (John Bradshaw, Bantam)
A classic self-help text. It's particularly useful for parents because it walks readers through each developmental stage from infancy through adolescence, helping them identify both specific emotional wounds and, more importantly, ways to heal the hurts within.

Unworried: A Life Without Anxiety (Dr. Greg Popcak, OSV)
Although this book offers a more general look at anxiety and anxiety disorders, the chapters on identifying and meeting needs (physical, emotional, spiritual, and relational), dealing with negative thoughts, and setting appropriate boundaries will be particularly helpful for parents — especially those who are anxious or self-critical about their abilities as a parent.

CatholicCounselors.com
Since 1999, our organization, the Pastoral Solutions Institute, has offered Catholic-integrated pastoral tele-counseling services for individuals, couples, and parents. If you need additional coaching/counseling services that respect your Catholic faith, we invite you to learn more about how we can help. Visit us at CatholicCounselors.com.

Prayer
Lord, help me embrace the priestly, prophetic, and royal aspects of my parenting role, so that I can heal the wounds that make it hard to love and be loved the way you want me to. Help me to consecrate every moment of my parenting life to you. Give me the grace to discover healthy, godly ways to meet my needs. Help me embrace your call to communion through loving service. Let me remember what it was like to be a child. Let me rest in your arms and fill me with your healing love so that I can give that same love to my kids. I give the broken parts of my heart to you. Make me whole in your love and grace.

Holy Family, pray for me. Amen.

Questions for Reflection

How does it change your perspective to think of Discipleship Parenting as a means by which God seeks to heal you as much as it is a way of raising godly kids?

In this chapter, we explored how parenting gives us the opportunity to develop the threefold mission of priest, prophet, and royal in baptism. How does this idea help you see the spiritual dimensions of parenting? How could this view help you connect more meaningfully with the ways God is trying to connect with you in your home — and specifically through your parenting role?

What personal needs are the hardest for you to meet on your own? How do you currently seek help meeting these needs? What more could you do to give yourself permission to identify your needs or seek others' help in meeting them in respectful ways?

Does the Four Questions Technique give you new insights into the aspects of parenting that are difficult for you?

What emotions would you like to address by using the Inside Out Exercise? How does viewing these feelings as other people change your relationship with these emotions?

CHAPTER 10

Astray Like Sheep: Discipling the Misbehaving Child

Do not provoke your children to anger, but bring them up with the training and instruction of the Lord.

Ephesians 6:4

Although we often stray from the fold, Jesus, the Good Shepherd, is infinitely patient with us. As much as this gives us comfort, sometimes it's hard to be patient with our little lambs when they're making trouble. Why do our kids misbehave, and how can we learn to respond as patiently as the Good Shepherd does with us?

Why Kids Misbehave: It's Not What You Think

Many people think that children misbehave because they're manipulative, willful, or bad. This view sets up an unnecessarily adversarial relationship between parents and children, in some cases even from infancy. One mom who brought her eight-year-old son to counseling told us, "He's always been a problem child. When I was pregnant, I was sitting on a fence. He kicked me so hard I fell off! I knew I was in for it from that

107

day on." This mother genuinely believed her child was out to get her before he was even born!

Although this is admittedly an extreme example, many Catholic parents buy into the idea that their children's poor behavior — even in infancy — is the result of their child trying to take advantage of them or manipulate them. It's important to note that this attitude is totally unsupported by both the traditional Catholic understanding of the person as well as science.

Protestant vs. Catholic View of Misbehavior

Sociologist Murray Strauss traced the idea that children misbehave because they're innately bad to the Calvinist (i.e., Presbyterian) belief in the "total corruption" of the person — the idea that people are born bad and stay bad even after they encounter Christ. This is a foundational tenet of Calvinist theology. America is a nation founded by Protestants, and most Americans still unconsciously operate on Calvinist assumptions about why people do what they do. Many parents — even Catholic parents — simply inherit this bias from the culture. As Cardinal Francis George once explained, Catholics in America are "Catholic in piety but Calvinist in worldview."

By contrast, the Catholic understanding of the child is best summarized by Servant of God Father Edward Flanagan (founder of Girls and Boys Town), who said, "There are no bad [children]. There is only bad environment, bad training, bad example, bad thinking." Catholics recognize that sin certainly impacts us, but we do not believe that anyone is either born bad or born to *be* bad. Yes, we're born with original sin, but baptism washes away the stain of original sin, leaving us pure and clean through God's grace. Although it's true that, even after baptism, human beings still struggle to do the right thing, the Church tells us that this struggle itself (called "concupiscence") is not sinful (see CCC 405).

What does all this philosophy have to do with parenting? Everything. Sin disrupted the original attachment that existed between God, man, woman, and humankind before the Fall, but at our core, we are still good (see Gn 1:31). By working to rebuild healthy attachment, we help our kids tap into their natural, God-given desire to be good.

In general, the more securely attached our children are, the harder they try to listen to us and to please us. The opposite is also true. The more insecurely attached our children are, the more they resist us and misbehave. Child development experts have a saying: "When children feel well, they behave well." Recall the eight brain-based skills associated with secure attachment. Research consistently demonstrates that healthy, happy, well-attached children are naturally empathic, kind, attentive, and obedient. Bad behavior is not a sign that the child is bad. It's a sign that the child is either hurting or that something is undermining the child's God-given desire to behave well.

In light of these insights, instead of speaking of children as "behaving" or "misbehaving," child development experts now speak of children as being "regulated" versus "dysregulated." More than antics with semantics, these terms actually refer to the way children's brains function when they're either behaving or misbehaving.

Building the Well-Behaved Brain

Think of the brain as a house with a basement, a first floor, and a second floor. The basement is the cerebellum, the *body brain*, which controls things like heart rate, respiration, and basic bodily functions. This is the most primitive level of the brain. The body brain is functional at birth, but it still needs some tuning up after birth to function at its best.

If we walk upstairs, the first floor of the mental house represents the limbic system, the *feeling brain*, which is responsible for emotions and desires, and responding to threats. The famous "fight, flight, or freeze" response is generated here too. The feeling brain is largely in charge during the child's first three years of life.

Up the next flight of stairs, on the top floor, we find the cortex, the *thinking brain*. This is the part of the brain that's mostly undeveloped at birth and will continue to mature into young adulthood. In a sense, the cortex is framed out at birth, but construction will need to continue throughout childhood and well into young adulthood. The cortex houses all of our life experiences as well as the lessons we learn along the way. Ideally, these lessons enable us to manage our emotions well, meet our needs appropriately, solve problems effectively, and apply the rules to real-life situations in healthy and creative ways.

When a child is well-regulated (behaving well) it means that these three parts of the brain are working well together. When this happens, in the face of a problem or stressor (e.g., hunger, sadness, fear, anger, excitement, confusion), the child can accomplish three tasks:

1. Identify how that problem/stressor is affecting his or her body (body brain)
2. Identify the emotional reaction to that problem/stressor (feeling brain)
3. Use the information he or she has learned to put all of his or her physical and emotional energy behind the best response to the problem (thinking brain)

When a child can do these three things, his mind is working properly. He can listen and behave.

By contrast, when a child is dysregulated, he behaves poorly. This happens, basically, for one of two reasons. First, one of the three "floors" of the child's "brain house" might be sagging or collapsing. For instance:

- The child is hungry, tired, uncomfortable, or sick (body brain problem).
- The child is overwhelmed with feelings of sadness, anger, fear, or confusion (feeling brain problem).
- The child doesn't know what to do in the first place — or understand how to apply what they already know — to a particular situation (thinking brain problem).

If any of these conditions exist, the dysregulated child will behave badly because they can't figure out the best way to meet a pressing need. For instance, a baby might frustrate the parent by crying and crying because she can't feed, change, or burp herself. This represents a meltdown (dysregulation) in the body brain.

Similarly, a toddler might tantrum because he doesn't have the language skills to talk himself through his feelings (feeling brain dysregulation). A middle school child might do something foolish because he or she can't figure out how to respond to this new (to him or her) challenge (thinking brain dysregulation). In this last instance, even though a parent may feel as though "I've told you a thousand times … " it can be hard for a child's developing brain to connect the dots. To most children, almost every situation seems new until they've gone through it a few hundred times — even if the "new" situation is similar to other things they've done before. The younger the child is, the truer this will be.

Can You Hear Me Now? Can You ... Ugh ...

The second reason children become dysregulated (i.e., behave badly) is that the "Wi-Fi" connecting the three floors is buffering too much. That is, the three parts of the brain might be having a hard time communicating with one another.

For example, how often have you been grumpy or sullen because you physically felt "off" but couldn't put your finger on why (i.e., bad connection between body and thinking brain)? Or how often have you felt sad, angry, nervous, or frustrated but couldn't imagine what you were so upset about (i.e., bad connection between feeling and thinking brain)? These experiences are caused by some kind of communication breakdown between the three parts of the brain. When we're regulated, the three parts of the brain are engaged in a metaphorical video chat, talking back and forth about what's happening in one another's lives and discussing how they might be able to work together to respond to it all effectively. But even if just one part's connection starts buffering, it prevents the whole brain from being able to figure out exactly what's going on or what the most effective response could be. Bad behavior results.

How often have you treated others poorly when you felt "off" or lashed out when your emotions got the better of you, even when you didn't know why? These are examples of times the different parts of your brain weren't communicating well. Think of how much harder it is for a child who doesn't have your skills or life experience.

In light of these examples, it's easier to appreciate that bad behavior isn't caused by a child's inability to refrain from being manipulative, willful, or defiant. Rather, children behave badly either because one part of their brain (body, feeling, or thinking brain) is wrestling with a problem it doesn't know how to handle *or* because the different parts of your child's brain are experiencing connectivity problems and, as a result, can't effectively coordinate their efforts.

This is especially true when a child is in a situation that *feels* new (even if it isn't). To find solutions to new problems, we need to apply the information we've already been given in new and creative ways. That takes communication between the three brains. When you ask your child, "Why did you do that?" and they stare at you blankly and say, "I don't know," they aren't lying. The panic they feel at being put on the spot makes their thinking brain shut down and their emotional brain take over. They *feel* shame, but they literally can't *think* well enough to explain why.

At this point, we'd like to take a moment to clarify a common point of confusion. When we use the term "dysregulated," we do not necessarily mean tantrumming, pouting, or melting down. A child is dysregulated any time they're not listening to you and following your directions. They might look perfectly calm. They may not even be pushing back. But assuming your child heard you and understood what you were asking, the normal response from a well-regulated child will be obedience. In fact, more often than not, it will be *cheerful* obedience. We don't mean that your child will necessarily be jumping with glee and asking for more chores, but assuming your child is well-regulated, you should normally expect to get a basically agreeable "OK, Mom" or "Sure thing, Dad." If you get anything less, there's most likely something that's at least slightly off in your child or in your relationship. You don't have to sound the alarm or call your therapist. But a sensitive and sincere, "Hey, buddy, you don't seem quite yourself. You doin' OK?" is probably in order. As Benjamin Franklin put it, "A stitch in time saves nine." Most parents think that they've got to wait until their child is so dysregulated that he or she is being openly defiant or losing it before they address it. If you feel ignored or get as much as an eye-roll, you should use the techniques in the next chapter to make an appropriate mini-correction and help you and your kid get back on track.

Regardless, when a child is dysregulated (i.e., behaving poorly) re-regulation (i.e., the return to appropriate behavior) occurs when a loving parent helps the child meet their need or figure out how to handle the new (to him) situation. We'll talk about how to do this in the next chapter. For now, it's just important to understand what our Catholic faith and science have to teach us about where "bad behavior" really comes from so that you can be prepared to respond to it ... gracefully.

Attachment and Behavior

No matter how securely attached a person is, we all struggle with dysregulation to some degree. We cannot perfect ourselves via purely human efforts.

That said, research does consistently show that how securely attached a person is will predict their ability to avoid becoming dysregulated in the first place or more quickly re-regulate when they've been knocked off balance. There are two reasons secure attachment facilitates a person's capacity for regulation.

Reason #1: Brain Discipleship

First, recall the House of Discipleship we described in chapter eight.

As your child grows into later toddlerhood and early childhood, and language begins to come online, you begin discipling your child's feeling brain by doing things like:

- helping them find the words to express their needs and feelings appropriately
- giving your child extravagant affection so that they can learn to re-regulate by synching up your more relaxed bodily rhythms to their own
- using gentle guidance and directed questions (not lectures) to help your child figure out the best way to respond to emotional situations
- creating household routines and family rituals that provide a safe structure to grow in

By doing this, you teach your child's feeling brain that you are the person your child should turn to for guidance in managing his or her emotions. *(Note: Even for parents who struggle with their own emotions, (a) this is good motivation to learn better tools [see the chapter on the healing powers of parenting] and (b) it would still be better for your child to come to you than learning these lessons from peers or forcing them to figure it out for themselves.)*

House of Discipleship

Stage Four: Relational Discipleship (Adolescence)

Teen turns toward parent to develop skills for having godly relationships and finding place in world.

Stage Three: Vocational Discipleship (Middle Childhood)

Child turns toward parent to discover and develop gifts in a way that helps him glorify God and make meaningful contributions to family and others.

Stage Two: Foundational Discipleship (Early Childhood)

Child turns toward parent to learn the stories, rules, and structures that lead to a love-filled, well-ordered life.

Stage One: Embodied Discipleship (Infancy and Toddlerhood)

Child turns toward parent to learn self-regulation and empathy through body-to-body communication.

In middle childhood and adolescence, you will focus more and more on discipling your child's thinking brain with practices such as:

- maintaining strong household routines and family rituals
- continuing to help your children find the words to express more and more complex emotions
- establishing ample one-on-one time to help your kids and teens apply the lessons they've learned to increasingly challenging personal and social challenges

At every step of the journey, the secure attachment fostered by Discipleship Parenting teaches the child how to identify and express their needs appropriately. Moreover, it establishes the parent as the child's go-to authority for meeting their physical, emotional, and cognitive needs in healthy, godly ways.

Reason #2: Building an Information Superhighway

The second way secure attachment facilitates good behavior is that it beefs up the "Wi-Fi" that connects the body brain, feeling brain, and thinking brain so that they can talk to one another more efficiently. By helping your child learn to stay calm, giving your child the vocabulary to express needs and feelings, and offering your child clear ways to consistently meet their needs, research shows that parents foster the growth of neural connections between the body, feeling, and thinking brains. These cognitive "information superhighways" facilitate more rapid and creative communication between the different parts of the mind.[1] This helps kids respond quickly and appropriately to various problems.

As we describe in our book *Beyond the Birds and the Bees*, making good moral decisions requires your child's brain to

- instantly apply the lesson they've previously learned to new situations;
- reflect simultaneously on what their feelings and needs tell them about that situation; and
- formulate a response that respects both of the above.

This process enables the child to offer consistent, heartfelt obedience instead of slavish, dutiful responses. In order to pull this off, the connection that links the different parts of the brain needs to allow instantaneous communication back and forth between the body, feeling, and thinking brains. Brain scans actually show how secure attachment creates these information superhighways. *Beyond the Birds and the Bees* describes this process in more detail as it relates to raising sexually whole and holy kids.

Dropped Connections

Unfortunately, the more insecurely attached a child is, the worse the "Wi-Fi" connection is between the different "floors" of the brain. For instance, anxiously attached people often struggle to hear their body brain at all. They don't do a good job of identifying when they need to sleep, eat, or otherwise take care of themselves. They don't tend to notice that they're falling apart … until they've fallen apart. They also exhibit spotty communication between the thinking and feeling brains. They may often feel anxious, insecure, and guilty, but have a very difficult time identifying why, much less knowing what to do about it.

Avoidantly attached people tend to be one giant thinking brain, with very little communication with their feeling brain and body brain. They're dutiful and driven, but their struggle to connect emotionally or see themselves as anything but "human doings" makes them susceptible to compulsive and addictive behaviors that numb their needs rather than meet them. Avoidantly attached people often lack insight. They attribute their problems, and even their emotions, to external factors because they struggle to have the internal dialogue that would allow them to understand what's going on inside them and how to fix it.

We share this to drive home two points. First, secure attachment is critical for helping the different parts of the brain communicate effectively so they can identify and meet their needs in moral and fulfilling ways. Second, parents with insecure attachment must do their best to address their own attachment wounds so that they can become the whole, healthy, godly, grace-filled people they were created to be and pass these lessons on to their children.

The Church's assertion that parents are co-creators of life with God does not begin and end at conception. The secure attachment that parents cultivate with their children facilitates the brain growth and regulation that's necessary for good and moral behavior.

In sum, children (and adults) behave badly when something is stopping the body brain, feeling brain, or thinking brain from functioning properly, or the connection between "floors" of the brain is spotty. When this happens, distraction, disrespect, and resistance result. By contrast, children (and adults) behave well because their body brain, feeling brain, and thinking brain are each functioning well in their own right and communicating effectively with one another. When a person's whole brain is functioning well, the default response is attentiveness, rapport, and a genuine desire to do the right thing.

Working to maintain strong attachment with your child helps you zero in on the factors that could be responsible for any dysregulation. Ultimately, this helps your child learn to stay regulated throughout the challenges of life.

Prayer

Lord, you have made me a co-creator of life with you. Help me to embrace that role at every stage. Give me the grace I need to form my child's mind so that their body, feelings, and thoughts can work together to glorify you.

Holy Family, pray for us. Amen.

Questions for Discussion

How does this understanding of the source of bad behavior challenge or confirm your own ideas about children's behavior?

Did it surprise you to learn that "dysregulation" refers to simple disobedience and not to tantrumming, pouting, or meltdowns? What difference does this insight make to your understanding of what you ought to be able to expect from your child and the quality of your relationship with your child?

What difference would it have made if your parents (both your mother and father) had viewed your misbehavior through the lens we propose in this chapter?

What healthy strategies do you use to re-regulate yourself when you become dysregulated?

What are some simple things you have done to successfully help your child re-regulate when they've become dysregulated?

• • •

Conclusion to Part Two

Discipleship discipline represents a radical shift in the way we think about managing our children's behavior. Instead of thinking of discipline as merely something we do to make kids behave and keep them out of our hair, discipleship discipline sees child-rearing as an ongoing relationship between a mentor (parent) and mentee (child), who are learning from each other and growing together in grace.

Just as the Salesians (the order of priests and religious founded by Saint John Bosco) view their founder's preventive system of discipline not only as a system of child-rearing, but also as a key element of Salesian spirituality, discipleship discipline is an integral component of an authentic Catholic family spirituality. It seeks not only to lead your child to God, but also to help you heal the wounds that might be preventing you from rejoicing fully in God's love for you, conveying that love to your children, and growing in the virtues that enable you to become a whole, healed, grace-filled, and godly person.

Discipleship discipline invites us to remember that we are not raising our children in our image, but in God's. Likewise it asks us to constantly reflect on how God may be speaking to us through the unique children he has given to us, and how he might be asking us to grow through our relationship with them.

Seen through the light of discipleship discipline, parenting — and discipline in particular — isn't merely a nuisance we have to deal with so that we can finally get around to other, more profitable, spiritual practices. It is the primary way we encounter God's love, hear his voice, discover his will, discern his call to growth, and learn how he wishes us to minister to our closest neighbors — our children.

PART THREE
Filling Your Discipleship Discipline Toolbox

*This system is all based on **reason, religion** and **loving-kindness**. Because of this it excludes every violent punishment, and tries to do without even mild punishments. … The practice of this system is all based on the words of St. Paul, who says: Love is patient, love is kind, it bears all things … hopes all things, endures all things (1 Cor 13:4–7).*

Saint John Bosco on The Preventive System of Discipline

What most parents consider discipline techniques are, in reality, punishments. Discipline is different from punishment. As Saint John Bosco taught, godly discipline is primarily concerned with teaching a child what to do and providing the structure, support, and practice necessary for the child to succeed. By contrast, parents with a more worldly, punishment-oriented mindset believe that if they just make a child's misbehavior too "expensive" (because of the inconvenience or pain the parent inflicts upon them), good behavior will spontaneously result. This punishment-oriented attitude represents the "repressive system" Saint John Bosco decried. It's also a terrible way to learn anything.

Imagine if your child's teacher spanked your child, or yelled at them, or made them stand in the corner, or took away recess every time they spelled a word incorrectly. Imagine further that when you complained, the teacher explained, "I TOLD them how to spell the word, but your child didn't listen. I had to give a consequence." You would, most likely, organize a march on the school with torches and pitchforks. And rightly so. Children don't learn *anything* — not math, spelling, punctuation, or especially good behavior — because someone tells them to do it (or punishes them for not doing it). They learn because someone reviewed the expectations clearly ahead of time and then provided the structure, support, and practice the child needs to succeed.

As we have asserted throughout this book, no matter how many tools you have in your toolbox, their effectiveness is directly related to the degree of attachment you have with your child. As the saying goes, "Rules without rapport leads to rebellion." You can't raise healthy, obedient children — much less godly ones — if you rely on punishments to make up for a poor or nonexistent relationship with your child. If you take this approach, you will either burn out, give up, lower your standards (because they're too difficult to maintain), or find yourself behaving more and more abusively. Your efforts will simply cause your child to become more sneaky, defiant, sullen, and rebellious.

That said, even parents who have an uncommonly good relationship with their children need good tools. The series of mini-chapters in this section (Part Three) will give you a brief overview of our most common techniques. Specifically, we'll look at the following techniques:

Rituals and Routines
Collecting
Team-Building
Catch Them Being Good
Virtue-Prompting
Do-Overs
Rehearsing

Time-In
Emotional Temperature Taking
Time-Outs (Making them work)
"Sibling Revelry"
Logical Consequences

Part Four will offer suggestions for applying these techniques in the various ages and stages of your child's development.

CHAPTER 11

Rituals and Routines

Rituals and routines are a critical part of discipleship discipline. Without them, every other technique becomes harder to employ and bears less fruit. Second only to secure attachment, family rituals and routines are essential for raising well-socialized, emotionally (and even physically) healthy children.

Rituals

The mission of Discipleship Parents is to raise kids who know how to live godly lives. By prioritizing daily opportunities to work, play, talk, and pray together as a family, Discipleship Parents model how Christians relate to work, leisure, relationship, and prayer.

Examples of daily family work rituals include things like:

- cleaning the kitchen together after meals
- picking up the family room together before bed
- folding laundry together
- cooking together
- doing light housework together

Examples of daily family play rituals include things like:

- playing cards or a board game together

- family story time
- playing outdoor games and sports as a family
- doing a family craft project

Examples of daily family talk rituals include things like:

- meaningful family mealtimes
- family meetings
- discussing the highs and lows of the day
- discussing ways to make you feel loved or cared for
- developing/reviewing a family mission statement

Examples of daily family prayer rituals include things like:

- grace before meals
- family praise and worship time
- P.R.A.I.S.E.
- blessing one another at the start of the day and before bed
- morning and bedtime family prayer
- attending Mass as a family
- family Rosary/chaplet

Daily, planned family rituals for working, playing, talking, and praying together are a catechism in Christian living. In our experience, the more an adult struggles to have work-life balance, enjoy appropriate recreational outlets, engage in intimate and meaningful conversations, and maintain a meaningful prayer life, the less likely it is they experienced the corresponding rituals in their homes growing up. Family rituals for working, playing, talking, and praying together strengthen the heart of your home and form well-rounded, godly kids.

Routines

In addition to family rituals, which tend to involve more meaningful family interactions, strong family routines enable you to effectively manage the details of the day-to-day life of your home. They involve simple activities like:

- getting ready in the same way/at the same time every morning
- getting to bed in the same way/at the same time every evening
- welcoming children home from school in the same way every day
- handling meal prep and chores in the same way every week

Consistent family routines create a sense of order and safety. They provide an environment where expectations are clear and good behavior can flourish. Strong household routines make it easier for kids to help with chores and be where they're supposed to be when they're supposed to be there. Not because you had to tell them, but because "that's the way it is" in your house, and it simply never occurs to them to question it. Strong family routines create an orderly current that flows through the house and carries everyone along with it. Without strong routines, parents are stuck deciding on the fly when and how things should happen and then trying to force the kids to conform to their will.

Creating strong family rituals and routines is as simple as it is countercultural. It starts by treating family time as the most important activity in the week and scheduling all other activities around it. Sometimes that means saying no to extracurricular activities. That's OK. Extracurricular activities should always *enhance* domestic church life, not compete with it. Some juggling between family rituals and extracurricular activities is always expected, but any activity that makes connecting as a family on a daily basis impossible needs to go. Never be afraid to tell coaches, teachers, or even your parish ministers that your children can't attend a particular practice, game, or event if it conflicts with a family ritual or stretches a family routine to its breaking point. Prioritizing your family life is an important way that your domestic church can evangelize the culture.

Because family rituals are such an important part of an authentic family spiritual life, we discuss this topic at length in *Discovering God Together: The Catholic Guide to Raising Faithful Kids*.

CHAPTER 12

Collecting

In order to get your kids to listen, you need to *collect* them first.
Imagine if a teacher walked into a classroom, picked up his briefcase, and as he walked back out of the room said over his shoulder, "Look kids, I have a ton of stuff to do today. I'll be back, but I need you to get all the problems on page thirty done. I'll check your work later" ... and then slammed the door and left. Would the assignment be completed? Would the teacher be justified in being upset when he came back and the majority of the students either failed to do the work or at least struggled to do it well?

It isn't unusual for parents to adopt a similar approach to discipline. Walking through the living room, we see our kid in the middle of some activity and say, "I need you to ... (clean your room, take out the garbage, take turns with your sister, etc.)," and then we wander off to do something else. We return later only to become outraged that the thing we asked for didn't happen.

Collecting helps avoid this by making sure your child is listening to you with their heart, not just their ears. It involves the following:

- Go to your child (or *gently and kindly* ask your child to come to you).
- Engage them/get their attention with affectionate contact.
- Communicate your expectation with a friendly tone. ("Hey,

buddy/honey, I need you to … ")

- Identify/resolve any problems that might stop the child from successfully completing the task.
- Ask them to repeat what they heard you say. ("Do you understand? OK, good. Now, tell me what I just asked you to do.")
- Be sure you actually see them start to do what you have asked them to do.
- Offer encouragement and let them know you're going to follow up.

Please note that these steps serve as a basic outline. The point of collecting isn't to follow a rigid template, but rather to walk the basic steps that will allow you to help your kids become regulated enough to follow through with what you've asked.

Here is an example:

Molly sees her son, John Paul (age six), playing with LEGOs in the family room. It's almost dinner time and she needs him to clean up. She goes to him **(Step 1 — Go to child)**, gets down on the floor, smiles at him, touches his arm **(Step 2 — Engage/Affectionate contact)** and says, "Whatcha doing, JP?"

"Makin' a time machine!"

"Wow, that's super cool! Where would you go in your time machine?"

"Back to the dinosaur times."

"You really like dinosaurs, don't you?"

"Yup!"

"Me too. Maybe we could go back to dinosaur times together after dinner. Would you like that?"

"Uh-huh."

"That sounds like a plan! Tell you what, though. We're going to have dinner in about ten minutes, so I need you to clean up your Legos." **(Step 3 — Communicate expectation)**

JP looks upset. "I thought you said we could play after dinner!"

"It's OK, buddy. We can. **(Step 4 — Identify and resolve obstacles)** How about I set your time machine on the bookshelf so it can be safe, and then you can put away all the loose Legos. If you need them later, we can take them back out. Do you understand?"

"Uh-huh."

"Great! So what's our plan?" **(Step 5 — Have the child repeat expectation)**

"You're going to put my time machine on the bookshelf so my sister can't break it, and I'm gonna put the other Legos away."

"That's right! Good job. Let's do it!"

Mom puts the time machine on the bookshelf and watches JP start to clean up. **(Step 6 — Observe the child complying)**

"You're doing a great job, JP. Keep it up. I have to go set the table, but I'll be back to see how things are going in about five minutes." **(Step 7 — Encouragement and promise to follow up)**

Your initial reaction might be, "That's great, but that takes a lot of thought and time." Honestly, though, if you reread the exchange between Molly and JP aloud, you'll see that it took about two minutes. That's a lot less time and energy than she would have spent if she just yelled from the kitchen, "JP, I need you to clean up and get ready for dinner!" and then ended up fighting with him ten minutes later when she returned to find nothing done. Yelling from the kitchen — or asking JP to clean up as she walked through the room — is "easier," but it almost always results in a frustrating outcome for the parent and the child. It is just one way parents give away their power.

You can also use collecting as a simple strategy to get things back on track when your child offers less than cheerful obedience. Here's one more example:

Jackie asked Tim (four) to get his pajamas on.

"I DON'T WANT TO!"

Jackie takes a breath and calms down. She sits down in front of him. "Wow. You really don't want to do what I asked, do you?"

"NO! I don't WANT to."

"I understand. It's really hard to do things you don't want to do, isn't it?"

"YEAH. I don't LIKE it!"

"I'm so sorry. I love you so much." (She holds him close to help him re-regulate, slowing his heart rate and helping him to breathe more deeply. After Jackie feels him relax into her arms [indicating that their bodies have synced up and they're in physical rapport], she continues to hold him as she stands up. Without drawing attention to it, she starts walking toward his bedroom. She says, "I just remembered: Tomorrow, you have a play date with Jeremy. What's your favorite thing to do when you play with Jeremy?"

"Superheroes!"

"That sounds like a lot of fun." She is now in his bedroom. "You know what? Superheroes use a lot of energy fighting bad guys. We need to make sure you rest up so you can be a super-duper bad-guy fighting machine! Which are better superhero pj's? Your blue ones or your red ones?

"The red ones!"

"Yeah, I thought so too." She starts helping him get his pj's on and continues talking about their plans for tomorrow.

In this example, Jackie refused to give away her power as parent by trying to convince Tim that he should want to put on his pj's. She simply recognized that he was dysregulated. She helped him re-regulate and provided a structure that helped him comply. What could have been the start of World War III in Jackie's house became a playful, intimate moment.

Collecting is a simple but powerful technique. You should be using it almost every time you ask your kids to do something — so about a thousand times a day. Collecting helps you make sure your kids are regulated and connected to you so that they can fully receive your instructions. As simple as this tool is, using it consistently will significantly increase the peace, order, and connection you enjoy in your household.

CHAPTER 13

Team-Building

Team-building is a technique that helps your kids clue in to the needs of everyone in the family. Team-building asks your whole family to consider how they can do a better job of taking care of one another during a particular block of time (e.g., morning routine, time between coming home from school and dinner, time from dinner to bed).

Team-building has three steps:

1. Identify the timeframe.
2. Ask how the family can take care of one another during that time period.
3. Create a concrete ritual to reinforce the change.

Here's an example:

Tina was frustrated with how chaotic things got when her four kids (eleven, ten, eight, and seven) came home from school. When the kids got home the next day, she asked everybody to come to the couch. She collected them (as described above) and got them to sit as close together with her as they could. She told them that she missed them and how glad she was to see them home, and asked a little bit about their day. Then she transitioned to the team-building exercise.

"Hey, listen, you know I've been frustrated lately about how crazy things get around here between when you come home from school and dinnertime. I was thinking: A family's supposed to be a team, and teams look out for one another, right?"

The kids agreed. Adam, the seven-year-old, got a little derailed. He started to talk about how his favorite team did at last night's game. Mom had to rein things back in.

"That's right, Adam. The Steelers had to really look out for one another to make that play, didn't they? Well, I was thinking that we need to be more like that. If we were going to be a better team, how could we work together to make sure we're taking care of one another between the time you come home and dinner?"

Together, they decide that after a light snack, they're going to either do homework, work on a project at the kitchen table, or help with some age-appropriate aspect of dinner prep. Mom suggested that they all take turns listening to one another's favorite music. Everyone liked that idea. They also agreed to take turns choosing a snack the night before so they all had something to look forward to.

Molly was pleasantly surprised by how on-board all the kids were. Sometimes she had to gently remind them of their plan, but overall, this approach led to a much more peaceful and enjoyable homecoming for all the kids. Based on their success, Molly and the kids decided to include Dad and make a plan for being a better team in the time between dinner and bedtime.

Every family has certain times during the day (or during the week) when they find it more difficult to get along. Instead of accepting this as a necessary downside to family life, use the team-building exercise to make a plan for having one another's backs when you need it most.

CHAPTER 14

Catch Them Being Good

It's easy to fall into the bad habit of exclusively pointing out when kids fail to meet our expectations. A much better approach is to "catch them being good," noting good behavior with small gestures of affection and affirmation. Studies consistently show that simple, positive reinforcement produces consistently better outcomes than punishments and consequences.[1] Your child wants nothing more than to see the light of approval in your eyes.

You don't have to throw a parade every time your child does something that pleases you, but remarking on good behavior lets them know that you're actually paying attention AND that you're glad to see them succeed. Here are some examples of catching kids being good.

- "I really like the way you guys are playing together. You're really good at sharing!"
- "It means so much to me when you just start picking up your toys on your own. I love how responsible you are."
- "I know that you're frustrated, but I see how hard you're trying to be respectful anyway. That really means a lot to me. Thank you."
- "I can see from the look on your face that your homework is really tough tonight. I really admire the way you're sticking with it. That's really impressive."

In each of the above examples, the parent remarked on a desirable behavior that occurred spontaneously and complimented the child for the virtue that the child was displaying. Doing this also helps you deal with times when your kids aren't behaving well. How? Because they'll know exactly what you mean — from experience — when you ask them to be "better sharers," or show more responsibility, respect, or stick-to-itiveness. They won't just understand the words. They will be able to relate to the specific behaviors associated with them because you took the time to punctuate their successes.

Some parents are concerned that this approach will spoil children or "give them a big head." Many parents who were raised in avoidantly attached households will especially struggle with this. For them, compliments were reserved for almost heroic feats. Anything less was just doing what you were supposed to do.

It is important to remember that spoiling is not caused by loving or complimenting your children or showing that you approve of them. It is caused by not encouraging children to be as generous to others as we are being to them. A child who is complimented and encouraged to sincerely and generously compliment others is not a spoiled child, but rather an affirmed, affectionate, and appropriately grateful child.

Likewise, please note that catching your child being good doesn't mean praising them for every breath they take. Catching your child being good simply asks you to consciously note the efforts your child makes to do the right thing. The Christian virtue of justice requires us to give a person their due. Acknowledging when our children behave well is nothing less than a matter of justice. We are simply giving them their due for having done their best to be their best.

When we catch our children being good, we imitate the Father in heaven who proclaimed to the crowds gathered by the Jordan, "This is my beloved Son, with whom I am well pleased" (Mt 3:17). Be like your Father in heaven and let your children know when you are well pleased with them.

CHAPTER 15

Virtue-Prompting

Rather than thinking for our children, it's important to help them develop their own consciences. Virtue-prompting is a simple exercise in which you ask leading questions to aid your child in identifying the virtues that can help them master a given situation. Here are two examples.

Child is upset because they didn't get the seat they wanted in the car. Mom says, "I understand that you're frustrated. What do you think the generous thing to do would be?"

Child sniffs, "Take turns?"

"That's a really good answer. So can you tell your brother that you're happy to let him have the seat this time if he will give you that seat next time?"

Child says to sibling, "You can have the window seat this time, but next time it has to be my turn, OK?"

"Nicely done, honey. I'm really proud of you. (Gives hug.)

• • •

Child (nine) is frustrated with his math homework. Dad notices and asks how he's doing. His son angrily huffs, "I'm FINE. What!?!"

139

Dad takes a breath to calm himself and says, gently, "I'm so sorry your homework has got you so upset. I see how burned out you feel, but can you think of a respectful way to tell me how you're feeling?"

Child puts his head in his hands and starts to tear up, "This is just so dumb. I'm never going to get this done."

Dad puts his hand on his son's shoulder. "I know how that feels. I'm really sorry. Wow, you feel really warm. Sometimes that happens when we get upset. How about we get you a cold glass of water and help you cool down?" Dad gets him the drink, and his son take a big gulp. "Better?"

"I guess. Yeah."

"Good. Tell you what, let's look at this together. Maybe it will go better with a little help."

"OK."

"I really appreciate your willingness to hang in there even when things are hard. That's really impressive. OK. Tell me what you've got."

•••

Many parents would respond to the behavior displayed in these two examples as challenges to their authority. They would then give away their power by trying to convince the child to do the right thing. Sensing the parent's weakness, the child would respond by doubling down, escalating things even further until the parent is either forced to give in or go crazy. Don't ever forget the following: It isn't your job to convince your child of anything. Ever. The only job you have is to set the *expectation* and facilitate *compliance* by enabling *regulation.*

In each of these examples the parents held on to their power by doing just that. They assumed that doing the right thing was a foregone conclusion. They just needed to help the child re-regulate by getting them to move out of their emotional brain and back into their thinking brain. By asking "What do you think the (responsible, generous, loving, respectful, etc.) way to handle (the situation) would be?" the parent teaches the child to face challenges with a solution-focused, virtue-based mindset. Ultimately, this helps the child concentrate more on seeking answers than wallowing in emotional reactions to problems.

CHAPTER 16

Do-Overs

Do-overs are exactly what they sound like. They give kids a chance to do things over the right way. This technique works best when a child has either rushed through a task and done a poor job of it or disregarded your attempt to virtue-prompt. When using do-overs, be careful not to just settle for the basic compliance. Focus on getting the right attitude as well as their best effort.

Here are some examples.

"You're so mean!"

"I understand that you're upset. Can you think of a way to express your feelings to me respectfully?" (Virtue-prompt attempt.)

Child rolls his eyes. In a semi-mocking, robotic voice, he says, "I feel upset, Moooooom. I am ve-ry sor-ry."

(Mom takes a breath. Reminds herself that this isn't defiance. It's dysregulation.) "I get that you're irritated about having to do it over, but I have all day if you need it. Try that again. I really do want to hear what you're upset about if you can tell me respectfully."

Child rolls his eyes again but uses a more civil tone. "I'm just really tired and I don't want to have to clean my room right now."

143

"Thank you, that was better. Can you try to tell me what you're asking me without rolling your eyes?"

Child takes a breath. Uses a reasonable tone. "Mom, I'm really wiped out from baseball practice. Could I clean my room some other time?"

"I really appreciate you asking me so respectfully."

In this instance, having gotten the child to re-regulate and approach you more respectfully, you could either choose to let him suggest another time to clean his room if you were actually 100 percent sure it would get done then, or you could gently insist that it be done now anyway. For instance:

> "I really appreciate you asking me so respectfully, and I would normally be open to your suggestion, but we have to go out after dinner and you won't have time to do it tomorrow. I know it's hard to do chores when you're tired, but thanks for being willing to do it anyway."

Again, notice that Mom retains her power by assuming that cleaning the room is a foregone conclusion. She doesn't ask whether it's OK if her kid cleans his room. She thanks him for doing it, even though it's hard.

Here is another example:

> You've asked your daughter to fold and put her clothes away. She acknowledges your request, and you see her take the laundry basket to her room. Later, you notice that her clothes are all stuffed in the drawers in a haphazard way. Some of them are hanging out of the drawers. You call her.
>
> "Honey, could you come here a second?"
>
> "What, Dad?"
>
> "I was really grateful when you said you would put your clothes away, but do you really think you gave the job your best effort?"
>
> "But I put them away!"
>
> "I know. I'm asking if you really gave your best effort to

what I asked you to do."

"Um … yesssss?"

(Dad says nothing. He just keeps looking at her.)

"Um … no?"

"Thank you for being honest. I agree. You can do a lot better. I need you to do this over. Please take everything out of your drawers, fold it properly, and put it away like you promised you would do in the first place. Do you understand?"

Her face is turning red and her eyes are watery. "Fine."

"Come here, Hon." Dad gives her a hug. "I know you're frustrated. Everybody is tempted to cut corners now and then, but I'm proud of you for being willing to do it right this time. I love you. I'll be back to check on you in half an hour."

Again, the father in this example was firm. He was clear about his expectations, and he didn't give away his authority by trying to argue with his daughter. He made it clear that he expected her best effort. Rather than lecturing her that she'd better do it right the next time or, worse, leave the clothes as they were but apply some unrelated punishment, he *expected* that she would do it right *this time*. He didn't try to talk her out of crying. He recognized that was just a symptom of the dysregulation. He was affectionate, firm, and showed that he was invested in her success by promising to come back and check on her progress in a reasonable amount of time.

Do-overs are not punishments. They are, however, good discipline. They're meant to be an opportunity for the child to do what you asked, do it right, and see that you can be pleased when they genuinely give you their best effort.

CHAPTER 17

Rehearsing

Rehearsing enables you to anticipate and head off potential problems. Telling kids to do something differently rarely works. When your child behaves poorly in a situation, rehearse a better response before walking into that situation again.

Here is an example:

You just parked in the grocery store parking lot. You remember that the last time you were in the store, your three kids kept running up and down the aisle, taking things off the shelf, and being disruptive. You decided that things would be different this time. You are instituting a "hold hands or hold the cart" rule. The kids need to either be holding your hand or holding onto the shopping cart. Before getting out of the car you say, "OK, kids. Remember we have a new rule. Who can tell me what it is?"

One of your kids remembers. She says, "We have to hold hands or hold the cart?"

"That's right. Everyone has to stay close so nobody gets lost and we can be a good team, so I need you either holding my hand or holding onto the side of the shopping cart the entire time we're in the store. We're going to practice by holding hands when walking through the parking lot."

"But you only have two hands!"

"You're right. Very smart. So I'm going to hold Jimmy's hand (the 4-year-old) and Ginny's hand (3-year-old) and you (6-year-old) can help me make sure Ginny stays safe by holding her other hand. Do you understand?"

"Uh-huh."

Jimmy pipes up, "But why can't I help keep Ginny safe?"

"You can! What a great big brother you are. If you hold my hand or hold the cart through the whole store to show me what a big boy you can be, you can help me keep Ginny safe by holding her other hand when we walk back to the car after we're done shopping."

You then take everyone's hand as discussed and walk to the grocery store. At the cart stand, you ask everyone to show you what they're going to do. The oldest two hold on to the side of the cart, and Ginny holds your hand.

"OK, guys, now one more thing. If you want to look at something, do you run away to look at it?"

"Noooooope!"

"That's right — what do you do?"

"We can say, 'Mom, can I see that?'"

"Excellent. But whether I say yes or no, what do you need to do?"

"Keep holding hands or holding the cart."

"What smart kids I have! Give me a big hug, guys! Great job. Ready? Let's do this."

The example also illustrates the "hold hands or hold you" rule that we strongly recommend that parents enforce. Children seven and under (and possibly older, depending upon the child's maturity level) should always be holding on to an adult any time they walk anywhere in public — indoors or outdoors. By religiously enforcing the "hold hands or hold you" rule from the time they learn to walk, you teach your children that wandering off on their own is not even a question.

Regardless, whether entering a store, anticipating problems before a playdate, taking your kids to church, or any other common arena for misbehavior, the rehearsing technique helps you anticipate possible problems and review solutions while you still have good control over the environment.

CHAPTER 18

Time-In

We'll talk about time-outs shortly, but long before you get to the point where you need to use time-outs, *time-ins* are a much more effective way to help your kids re-regulate.

Remember, poor behavior is caused by dysregulation. Dyregulation occurs when a child is struggling to meet their needs, apply their skills, or manage their emotional temperature. Children under three years old have virtually no ability to self-regulate. They're almost entirely dependent upon Mom and Dad's body to help kickstart their own body's capacity for self-regulation.

Children three to six have some limited capacity for self-regulation due to their increased language ability. Chances are, you use a great deal of self-talk to calm yourself down. ("It's going to be OK. Just take a deep breath.") Kids aren't capable of self-talk until they've mastered speech and have a basic emotional vocabulary. That's why three- to six-year-olds are somewhat better than toddlers at managing emotions. They have more words.

Children over seven should have a basically well-developed capacity for self-regulation. At the very least, children seven and older should have outgrown most tantrums. Prior to age seven, tantrums tend to be genuinely related to being overwrought, while tantrums after seven are almost always more manipulative in nature.

Regardless, the struggles that all children have managing their emotions come down to losing control of whatever ability they have to re-regulate after a stressful, exciting, or overwhelming experience. Notice we included "exciting" in this list. That's because children can go from being wildly happy to melting down in tears in a heartbeat. Excitement causes similar boosts in adrenaline to stress. It's all stimulation. Re-regulation is the process by which the body learns how to reset itself after being overstimulated for any reason — even good reasons. That's where the time-in technique comes in.

Time-in is similar to collecting in that it relies on increasing your child's connection with you to help them get their emotions back under control. The difference is that while collecting happens *before* a child seems stressed or upset, time-ins happen when you notice that your child seems "off." Time-in consists of affectionate, one-on-one time with your kids that helps them reengage the "calm-down system" in their brain (the parasympathetic nervous system). Here is an example:

Your 5-year-old son has been running around and having a great time playing with Dad. You said that he will need to get ready for bed soon, and your five-minute warning seems to have registered. Still, when you say that it's time to get ready, he screams out, "NO!" You're immediately tempted to start yelling and turning the exchange into a power struggle, but you remember that he is probably dysregulated from having so much fun and that he needs some help transitioning.

You get down on the floor. You and your husband start by empathizing with him. "You're having a really good time with Dad and you don't want to stop, do you?"

"NO!"

"I totally get that. Dad's super fun, isn't he?"

"Yeah!"

"I'm glad you think so too. Can you and Dad tell me all about what you were playing?"

Your son comes over. You set him on your lap and ask him to tell you about their game. Your husband and your son take turns telling the story. As they talk, you can see your son relaxing a bit. You say, "Wow. That sounds like a really fun game!

Maybe you guys could play some more tomorrow. Would you like that?"

"Yeah!"

"That's awesome. Hey, I have a great idea! Let's talk about all the other things you'd like to play tomorrow while we get your jammies on." The three of you start walking toward your son's bedrooom while he describes some of his other favorite games.

Notice that instead of turning this into a fight, Mom and Dad employed empathy and affection to help their son calm down and transition into getting ready for bed.

Another way to use time-in is when you notice a general shift in how much your children are pushing back against your authority. Sometimes, no matter how effective you are as a parent, your relationship with your kids seems a little strained. Not bad. Just, not quite right. In addition to whatever consequences or strategies you might use to keep basic order, this sense of resistance you are getting from your children is almost always a sign that you could benefit from some time-in. In this case, time-in might involve special one-on-one time doing a project together, going for breakfast or dessert, or engaging in some other enjoyable — but not too stimulating — activity that helps you get back in sync with each other. Here is an example.

Let's say that you've needed to correct a particular child more than usual in a given week. Thinking about it, you realize that you haven't gotten a lot of one-on-one time lately. You continue to put out the little fires as they come up, but you also start planning to get some time together. You invite your child to go to breakfast on Saturday. During breakfast you make a point of making the time as pleasant as possible. You let your child lead the conversation. You show genuine interest in what they're saying. You ask questions. You let them teach you about their life and interests. About three-quarters through your time together, you mention that you've noticed that things have seemed a little "off" between the two of you lately. Without going into lecture mode, you mention a few examples just to illustrate what you mean.

Next, you ask whether something has been bothering your child. You mention that sometimes kids have a hard time being cooperative when they feel frustrated about something, but they don't know how to say it. You ask if there is anything that they need to talk through, and you listen patiently as they explain any concerns.

Using the team-building strategy we outlined earlier, you identify ways to work together better in those situations the next time they come up. Once that's done, you thank your child for being willing to work through this and tell them how proud you are of them for being so grown-up. You spend the last few minutes of your time-in talking about something more pleasant so you can end on a good note.

In this variation on the time-in strategy, you're intentionally making a deposit in your child's emotional bank account so that, when you ask for their obedience, they don't respond as if you've overdrawn your account. Some parents react negatively to time-in. They feel like they're being asked to reward their child's bad behavior. This attitude is based on the assumption that kids are naturally inclined to do bad things and be annoying. Remember, neuroscience tells us that the *normal state* of a well-attached, well-regulated child is compliance. If a child is having consistent problems behaving well, that means something is threatening the attachment between the parent and child, or the child is struggling to deal with something that's making him feel overwhelmed or overwrought. Time-ins address both of these concerns by strengthening your attachment and allowing you to help your child address whatever might be upsetting them. By doing this, you reinforce your discipleship relationship by sending the message, "There is nothing I am unwilling to help you through — even problems with me." Communicating this via consistent use of time-ins is much more effective than simply saying, "You can tell me anything" and then wondering why your child doesn't.

CHAPTER 19

Emotional Temperature-Taking

The emotional temperature-taking technique gives both you and your children a way to consciously recognize when they are in danger of becoming dysregulated. Once you've got the basic idea, the technique is almost infinitely adaptable.

Imagine a scale that goes from 1 to 10, with 1 representing completely calm and regulated and 10 representing completely dysregulated. A 6 represents the times we discussed in the last chapter when your child just feels "off" even though, outwardly, things seem fine.

The scale is not based on your own or your child's impression of how they feel. *It's based on how they're behaving.* Also, please note, a higher emotional temperature does not mean that the child is necessarily tantrumming or melting down. Some kids get quiet and withdrawn.

Many different things cause one's emotional temperature to escalate. A high emotional temperature could mean that your child is overwhelmed and upset, but it could just as easily mean that your child is happy but completely overstimulated by a particularly crazy playtime. The child may also be hungry, tired, or sick. Don't assume that, because your child isn't tantrumming, they're fine. Use the following behavioral symptoms to gauge your child's emotional temperature. You might also find yourself in these descriptions.

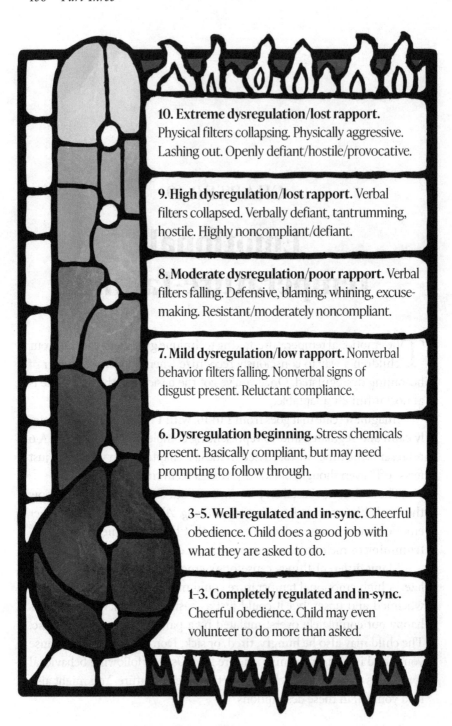

10. Extreme dysregulation/lost rapport. Physical filters collapsing. Physically aggressive. Lashing out. Openly defiant/hostile/provocative.

9. High dysregulation/lost rapport. Verbal filters collapsed. Verbally defiant, tantrumming, hostile. Highly noncompliant/defiant.

8. Moderate dysregulation/poor rapport. Verbal filters falling. Defensive, blaming, whining, excuse-making. Resistant/moderately noncompliant.

7. Mild dysregulation/low rapport. Nonverbal behavior filters falling. Nonverbal signs of disgust present. Reluctant compliance.

6. Dysregulation beginning. Stress chemicals present. Basically compliant, but may need prompting to follow through.

3–5. Well-regulated and in-sync. Cheerful obedience. Child does a good job with what they are asked to do.

1–3. Completely regulated and in-sync. Cheerful obedience. Child may even volunteer to do more than asked.

From 1 to 3 on the emotional temperature scale ...

Your child is completely in sync with you and almost perfectly well-regulated. At this level, they're affectionate, unusually empathetic, and capable of both cheerful obedience and willingly going above and beyond what you have asked them to do. You shouldn't expect your child to be in this range all of the time, but it should at least be a semi-regular occurrence in a well-attached household with good rituals and routines.

Between 3 and 5 on the emotional temperature scale ...

You and your child are in sync with each other, and your child is very well-regulated. At this range your child is capable of doing what you ask with a good attitude; although, as you get closer to 5, your child might need a little extra prompting to prevent them from getting distracted and to follow through as well as they should.

At 6 on the temperature scale ...

Your child is able to be compliant, but it's obvious that it's requiring a little more effort for them to do so. At this temperature, your child may seem a little distracted, tired, or frustrated. This is because stress chemicals like cortisol and/or adrenaline are beginning to drip into their bloodstream. At this level, your child will respond to you, but you might have to ask more than once to get their attention. Things just seem "off." This would be a good time to use some basic collecting and time-in techniques to help your child reconnect with you and re-regulate himself or herself before sending your child off to do whatever you asked. At this temperature, collecting is more of a preventive tactic and shouldn't take more than a minute, but the investment is time well spent.

At 7 on the emotional temperature scale ...

Stress chemicals are building up in your child's brain and bloodstream, shutting down the nonverbal behavior filters in their brain. A child at a 6 or lower doesn't roll their eyes, huff and puff, fidget, grimace, or have a hard time looking at you when you're talking to them. At a 7, however, the brain-based self-control mechanisms that would normally prevent these behaviors are going offline. At this temperature, your child will have a hard time not showing outward signs of disgust, irritation, or frustration about almost anything. If you see these behaviors, don't take them personally. They have nothing to do with you. Your child is effectively being poisoned by his own brain chemistry. He may be tired, hungry, frustrated, or otherwise wound up for some unknown reason. That doesn't justify disobedience, but it's a reason to pause, collect your child, and/or give him or her some time-in.

At a 6, collecting and time-in were preventive. At a 7, you will use those techniques to reset your child, as they are beginning to go off track. If you become heated yourself, you will most likely trigger a major disruption. Instead of giving away your power by fighting your child, hold on to it by offering up a quick prayer, controlling your own reactions, and helping your child re-regulate. Use collecting and/or time-in to get your child back down to a 5 before sending your child to do what you need them to do. It may take two to three minutes at this stage, but it's worth the effort.

At 8 on the emotional temperature scale ...
Your child is strongly "under the influence" of the stress chemicals in their bloodstream. Your child's nonverbal filters have now collapsed. Their verbal filters are under attack. Your child isn't yelling, screaming, or openly defiant, but they will be whiny, defensive, blaming, begging, and saying things like, "Do I haaaaave tooo?" and "it's not FAAAIIIRR!" Some children may start tearing up or go very quiet, sullen, and unresponsive. Again, assuming your request is developmentally appropriate, it's never a question that your child needs to do whatever you ask him or her to do. But if you see your child behaving this way, collecting and/or basic time-in will be critical. Plan on this taking five to ten minutes. That may feel inconvenient, but if you try to push your child past this point without collecting him or her first, you will most likely provoke a major tantrum that will exhaust both of you.

At 9 on the emotional temperature scale ...
Your child's verbal filters have fallen. They're officially melting down, saying mean things, starting to tantrum, and/or being openly defiant. Alternatively, some children will just shut down. They won't say anything mean, but they won't do what you asked, and they won't be able to answer

your questions. They will just stare at you, crying and saying, "I don't know," over and over again. At a 10 your child is officially out of control. Their nonverbal, verbal, and physical filters have collapsed. They're now hitting, throwing, or fighting with you on top of everything else.

Please note, none of these behaviors are, technically speaking, defiant. They're signs of a high level of dysregulation — of being poisoned by their own stress chemicals. You should attempt collecting/time-in at this stage, but the chances are good that your child will resist you. If your child is willing to stay with you, it may take ten to fifteen minutes before your child is re-regulated. Even then, your child may act a little emotionally "hungover" from all the stress chemicals they had surging through their body. As the parent, your goal is, ideally, to consistently intervene long before your child gets to this stage on the emotional temperature scale.

Every child gets to a 9 or 10 occasionally, but if your child constantly seems to be at a 9 or 10, you will either need to clue in much sooner to your child's emotional temperature, learn to do a much better job of managing your own emotional temperature (because you can't teach your child what you don't practice yourself), or you may need to address a more chronic health or attachment issue.

Again, at a 9 or 10, you can attempt collecting or time-ins, but if your child is older than three, you may need to use the strategies we will describe below as well.

In addition to using this temperature chart to know when and how to intervene, we recommend teaching your child to identify their emotional temperature and helping them learn to ask you for a hug, or some time-in, or help finding a calming activity to do when they need to re-regulate. Make a colorful chart with different faces representing the points on the scale. Have your child draw pictures of things they can do at each point to lower their temperature. Post the chart where your child can see it. When they seem "off" to you, ask them to check the chart and tell you their temperature throughout the day so they can learn to monitor their own emotional well-being. Children as young as three or four can be taught to do this (though not younger). Learning to self-regulate is a critical lesson to learn and master in early and middle childhood.

One last note on the emotional temperature scale. Some parents indicate that their children go from "a zero to a 10." This is true of infants and toddlers, as they simply do not have the brain capacity to self-regulate. Parents need to do all the heavy lifting to help infants and toddlers re-regulate with lots of affection and time-in. This body-to-body interaction time helps little ones learn the basics of self-soothing by early childhood.

That said, children three and up who exhibit this tendency to rapidly escalate are most likely operating at a 7 to 8 all of the time without you realizing it. They escalate quickly because they are always just shy of exploding, and they don't have the emotional bandwidth to handle any additional stressors. If this describes your child, begin looking at the bigger picture for what might be causing your child to live at such a high stress level. Do your best to identify and address those issues to lower the baseline emotional temperature. If you are unsuccessful in identifying or resolving these problems, seek professional help.

CHAPTER 20

Time-Outs (Making Them Work)

Frankly, 99.9 percent of parents do time-outs incorrectly. Sending your child to his room (or to a step, or the corner) and expecting your child to become well-behaved after spending a few minutes there by themselves isn't discipline. It's a magic trick. Children do not go away and come back "better." How is that supposed to work? Does the Good Behavior Fairy come and smack sense into them when you're not looking? (Hint: The correct answer is no.) When parents complain that time-outs don't work, this is why.

There is a way to do time-outs that actually works. A few qualifications first: You should never use a time-out on a child younger than three and preferably not on a child younger than five. You can make a 3-year-old sit in place, but they will learn nothing from it. By the time you let them up, they've most likely forgotten why you put them there in the first place. Collecting, time-ins, do-overs, rehearsing, team-building, and the like are much more effective up until the age of six.

Likewise, time-outs should never be your go-to, first-line strategy. Time-outs should only be used when the child is at an 8 or higher on the emotional temperature scale, and then *only* if they actively fight your attempts to help them re-regulate by collecting them or using simple time-in strategies.

Here are the steps to an effective time-out:

1. Attempt to collect the child.
2. Take the child to time-out.
3. Visit the imprisoned.
4. Have a "parole hearing."
   - What did they do wrong?
   - Sincere apology
   - Identify alternative behavior
   - Role-play/practice
5. (If your child fails their "parole hearing") Rinse and repeat.

Let's walk through this together.

1. Attempt to collect the child

Before you send your child to time-out, try to help them re-regulate. If you're successful, then proceed to the do-over, rehearsing, or other strategy, or simply redirect the child to do what you asked in the first place. That said, if the child is between an 8 and 10 on the emotional temperature scale, there is a good chance your attempts to help them calm down will actually inflame the situation. They're overstimulated. The equivalent is when you're upset and someone tries to give you a hug, only to have you say, "DON'T TOUCH ME!" Children get to this place much more easily. If your child is at this place, say, "I am trying to help you calm down, but if you don't want my help, I will have to give you a time-out to get yourself under control." Give them an honest choice between getting your help and giving them the space to work through things in time-out.

A time-out is not meant to be a punishment (even if your child acts like it is). It's an opportunity to give the child a quiet place to get back down to at least a 6 so that you can help them calm down the rest of the way and learn how to better handle the situation that landed them in trouble.

2. Take the child to time-out

If you need to send your child to time-out, don't argue with them. Lead them by the hand or carry them to a safe, quiet place where they can sit by themselves for a time (usually one minute per year of age to start). This space should have few distractions and no toys or devices. It should also not be their bedroom. A spare room or guest bathroom (with no cleaning supplies the child can use to harm themselves) is a good go-to. If the child starts saying, "I'm calm! I'm calm!" on the way to the time-out, they're not calm. It's too late. They MUST complete the time-out once you have made the call.

3. Visit the imprisoned

"Visiting the imprisoned" is a *Corporal Work of Mommy* — um, that is, mercy. Here is your chance to practice this merciful work. Your child should never just come out of time-out on their own, "when they're calm." Chances are good that if your child got to a 9 or 10, they will be a poor judge of when they're actually re-regulated. Some parents complain that their child is in time-out all day. This is usually because the child "calms down" to a 7 or 8 on the emotional temperature scale, but then keeps being re-triggered the rest of the day. The child must stay put until you come to check on them when their time is up.

4. Have a "parole hearing"

The child does not immediately get to come out when you go to get them. Instead, they get a kind of "parole hearing" to test how re-regulated they really are.

- Gently ask them to tell you what they did wrong.
- Ask the child what they could have done differently. Younger children will need help with this step, but even they should be able to demonstrate that they've given real thought to this question and be able to offer at least a few reasonable ideas. Older children should be held to a higher standard.
- Ask for a sincere apology (emphasis on sincere). You can tell the difference between an "I'm truly sorry" apology and a "this is what you want me to say" apology. You need the real thing.
- Role-play the situation. Give them a chance to practice

showing you that they can do it right next time. This is the
most important step because it gets the new behavior into
your child's muscle memory. *If you skip this step, everything
you have done to this point was wasted.*

If they successfully role-play with you, then hug them and praise them
for working through it. Let them know that you are proud of them for
getting control of themselves enough to work through this with you. Assuming they've completed all the steps of this process successfully, they
should be at least a 4 or 5 and safe to be let back into society.

5. Rinse and repeat

If your child cannot do one or more of the above steps sincerely and to
your satisfaction, their emotional temperature is still too high. Require
them to stay in time-out for another round. Check back in on them again
at the end of their time. Repeat as necessary for as long as is necessary.
You MUST not let your child out of time-out until they've sincerely and
successfully completed the previous four steps. Letting your child out
early simply teaches them to wait you out. They will, eventually, come
to believe that the only reason that you put them in time-out is because
you are "mean" and only apply consequences because you're angry. Discipline isn't about addressing your irritation. It is about changing your
child's behavior. Stick with it until you get the change you're looking for.

CHAPTER 21

Sibling Revelry

We often hear about sibling rivalry, but how can you cultivate "sibling revelry" — that is, the ability for brothers and sisters to stop fighting and learn to respect one another and enjoy one another's company?

The sibling revelry technique is similar to the steps of time-out, only it is used with two or more children simultaneously. When your children (six or older) are bickering, rather than trying to decide who did what to whom or whose side to take, use the following steps to foster sibling revelry.

1. Virtue-Prompt

When you hear the children bickering, give them a minute to see what happens. If you hear things start to escalate, don't yell. Use virtue-prompting. Say something like, "Hey kids, it sounds like this would be a good opportunity for you both to practice (generosity, respect, kindness, etc.). See if you can figure out how without me."

2. Modified Time-Out

If things continue to escalate, send both children to separate spaces. They will remain there for the usual amount of time (one minute per year of age) with the mission to "Think about what you did to make the situation worse, and what you could have done to make it better."

This reflection eliminates the "Who started it?" debate. In every exchange, no matter who is more responsible, each person has the power to make things better or worse. This process will help you teach your child that they always have the power to make a positive difference, even when they feel thwarted or frustrated.

When it is time for their "parole hearing," visit each child in turn. Often, the first time through, kids continue to complain about what the other child did. If that happens, give them another turn in time-out with the same request. Repeat until they can tell you what they needed to do differently, or until you can see that they have made a genuine effort but really cannot figure it out on their own. In that case, work out alternatives together.

When each child has identified what they could have done to make things better, bring the kids back together. Have them work the following steps.

- Say what they personally did wrong (with no qualifications).
- Give each other a sincere apology.
- Say what they will do in the future.
- Role-play, under your supervision, these healthier alternative responses.

If either child struggles to do any of these things well, send them back to time-out until they are ready to do them. If one child is genuinely contrite earlier, it's OK to let them out of time-out and bring them back to complete the final steps when their sibling is ready.

When all the children have completed the process, praise them for their hard work. Take a moment for a genuine group hug and send them on their way.

Remember, time-outs and sibling revelry are only for those situations where your children cannot be calmed and redirected in simpler ways. It's always preferable for the parent to be able to work through things instead of having to send your kids away. It's fine if you have to resort to time-outs and sibling revelry *occasionally*. If you find yourself using them every day, or even several times a week, something is wrong with your approach. You may benefit from some parent coaching from our tele-counseling service. Learn more at CatholicCounselors.com.

CHAPTER 22

Logical Consequences

The final discipleship discipline technique we will explore is logical consequences. A consequence is not a punishment. Punishments simply impose (often random) inconveniences or pain on the child in the belief that if the child suffers enough for doing "bad" things, they will spontaneously learn to do "good" things.

As opposed to punishments, logical consequences create a system whereby the child must consistently demonstrate good behavior in order to earn — or earn back — a privilege that was abused. Logical consequences are never random, and they're not all that creative. They're tied directly to the offense, and they lead directly to the desired appropriate response. Here are some examples of logical consequences at work.

Tim, nine, consistently struggled to stop playing his video game. At first, his parents tried helping with the transitions. They would give him a fifteen-minute warning and then let him know again in ten and five minutes when he needed to turn it off. This approach had worked with his older brother, but it was not working with Tim. Eventually, rather than arguing with him, his parents would have to turn off the TV and make Tim stop playing. This resulted in him pitching a fit. He would calm down after a time-out. He was always sorry and he always knew what he should do, but he couldn't make himself do it in the situation. His parents decided to use a logical consequence.

They explained the rule: "In this house, we always work hard to love people more than things. But by acting the way you do, you are loving your games more than you love us, and that's not OK. We want you to be able to play your video games, but only if you are mature enough to show us that you can love people more."

Tim's parents explained that he was *not* going to be allowed to play any video games for a week. During that week, they were going to use the virtue-prompting and team-building strategies to help him think of ways he could show his family that he loved them more than he loved himself or his things. That included behaviors like remembering to do his regular chores without being told, cheerfully doing what he was asked the first time, and taking it upon himself to volunteer help when he saw his parents or siblings were doing a chore.

The family would remind him about this deal every day when he woke up and gently redirect him if he struggled. They would not add to his consequence during this time if he struggled, but they would keep track of his progress.

At the end of the week, Tim would meet with his parents. They would decide whether he had done his best to show that he loved people more than his things. If he made a genuinely sincere effort, he would be allowed to have the game back with the understanding that he would need to continue to show that he loved his family more than his games. On the other hand, if he did not make a good effort, or if he continued to whine, pout, or fight to get his game back instead of working to show that he loved his family more than his games, then when they met at the end of the week, Tim's parents would give him another week without the games to practice loving people more than things.

This approach eventually helped Tim learn to enjoy technology in a responsible, family-centered way.

Here is another example:

Jenna, six, was always late getting ready in the morning. Even after her parents tried several more gentle strategies to help her be on time, she still resisted. Jenna's parents decided to apply a logical consequence. They gave Jenna time to practice getting ready for school on time. On Friday evening, they explained that instead of letting her sleep in the next morning, she would be getting up at her usual time so that she could practice getting ready for school. On Saturday morning, Mom and Dad woke Jenna and coached her through her morning routine. They used a stopwatch to time her as she went to the bathroom, brushed her teeth, showered, and got dressed. All the while they adopted the persona of a positive, slightly insane athletic coach as they cheered her through her morning routine and counted her down to the next activity until she was clean, dressed, had her books, and was standing at the door waiting for the bus.

Then they had her go back to her room, get back into her pj's, climb into bed, and run the drill again. At the end of the second run-through, they congratulated Jenna on getting ready on time. They explained that they expected her to be on time every morning, or next Saturday they would run the "getting ready for school drill" at least three times until she could prove that she knew what they wanted her to do and could do it consistently. They promised to do this every Saturday until she could show them that she had the skills to get ready consistently every weekday morning.

Here is one last example of using logical consequences:

Eric, eight, was not doing as well in his classes as his parents expected he should be based on past performance. He was missing assignments and turning in sloppy work. His parents talked to his teacher and found that he was keeping up in class. He seemed to understand the assignments; he was just doing poorly with homework.

Because he had done well previously, his parents had gotten out of the habit of reviewing his work. They realized that once they stopped checking in on him, he interpreted that as a sign that they didn't care what he did. That evening, they explained that because it was important to them that Eric do well in school, they were going to make some changes in the way he approached homework. They wanted to make sure that they were available to him in case he had questions, so from now on, he was to do his homework at the kitchen table. Likewise, they explained that regardless of his teacher's expectations, their expectations were even more important. They informed Eric that they would be checking his homework not only to see that his answers were correct, but also to make sure that his work was done neatly and showed that he cared about what he was doing. If not, they would ask him to do it over.

They did not lecture him. They were calm and pleasant when they explained the new routine. When he whined and begged them to just let him do it in his room, they empathized with him and told him they understood how frustrating it was for him to have to make this change. They didn't try to convince him to see things their way. They explained that this is the way it was going to be, and they let him have his feelings about it. The next night they started their new homework routine.

The first week was a little tough for everyone, but by the second week, Eric was doing his work at the kitchen table without complaint. He seemed to actually appreciate the extra help and attention he was getting, and he was proud that his grades were improving. With time, he took more responsibility for his work and was allowed to work in his room, but his parents continued to review his work with him both for correctness and neatness. Eric learned to care about his work because his parents cared about it even more — without suffocating him in the process.

We will offer a few other examples of logical consequences in the age-appropriate chapters of this book. For now, it's enough to know that logical consequences are not meant to punish a child (even when they react as if it's a punishment). Rather, logical consequences create a structure that enables success.

• • •

Conclusion to Part Three: Closing the Toolbox

Discipleship Parents don't waste their time coming up with ever more creative ways to force their children to submit to their authority. Instead, they look for ways to create peaceful, orderly interactions within the household that help facilitate the brain-based regulation that's necessary for children to learn and grow in virtue. Discipleship Parents follow Saint John Bosco's example of training children through the use of "reason, religion, and lovingkindness." They aren't interested in being enforcers or police officers. Rather, Discipleship Parents see themselves as loving shepherds of their children, committed to using every encounter to create more loving, joyful households, and more generous, loving, virtuous kids.

Prayer

Jesus, you are my Good Shepherd. Help me lead my little sheep to you with the same gentleness, mercy, kindness, and love with which you shepherd me. Let me be like you, "slow to anger, abounding in mercy." Help me to love and guide my children down the right paths in a manner that shows them how to be good out of love, not fear. And help me to always remember that discipline is not something I do to my children or techniques I use on my children, but a relationship I have with my children that fills their hearts with your love and makes them want to share that same love with others.

Holy Family, pray for us! Amen.

Discussion Questions

How did the techniques in Part Three challenge your ideas about what effective discipline entails?

How does the approach to discipline outlined in these chapters differ from the way your parents raised you?

How could this approach to discipline improve your relationship with your kids?

Which of the techniques described in Part Three do you already use? Which would you like to become more effective with?

What behaviors would you most be interested in helping your children overcome? Which of the techniques do you think would be most helpful and why?

PART FOUR
Discipleship Parenting for the Ages (and Stages)

In this final section of *Parenting Your Kids with Grace*, we'll look at what it takes to disciple your children at each age and stage: from infancy (birth to twelve months), through toddlerhood (twelve to thirty-six months), early childhood (three to six), and middle childhood (seven to ten).

You'll discover how to parent gracefully through the challenges of each stage, apply the ideas we've discussed to specific discipline challenges, and help your children meet their needs in godly ways so that they can experience their Catholic faith as the path to a healthy, fulfilling, joyful life.

While you may prefer to zero in on the chapters that focus on the ages of your own children, we encourage you to also look at the chapters that discuss the stages immediately before and after. Developmental stages are somewhat fluid. Some of the information discussed in an earlier stage will most likely apply to your child. Likewise, the information discussed in the subsequent chapter will give you a better sense of the goals you are parenting toward.

We hope the following chapters will be a blueprint for building your House of Discipleship with grace and confidence.

CHAPTER 23

Discipling Your Infant

Before I formed you in the womb I knew you,
before you were born I dedicated you ...

Jeremiah 1:5

Babies are amazing. They are also completely dependent. Saint John Paul II's Theology of the Body offers hints that there's a divine reason babies aren't born ready to take care of themselves. Having needs forces us to turn to others. Sin attempts to separate and isolate us, but human beings were created for communion. Before the Fall, human beings' neediness in infancy would have served as an invitation to participate in the communion for which we were created. After the Fall, that same neediness serves as an invitation to heal from the separation and isolation sin inflicts on us. Seen in this light, our baby's cries are not a nuisance. They are a primal and prophetic call to communion. God created human children to be "needy" not to inconvenience parents, but so that he could build the call to communion into our very DNA. Babies are meant to be needy, and parents are meant to respond to their needs — promptly, generously, and consistently. By nurturing attachment, parents heal the alienation sin wants to create in our families — the very foundation of society.

Babies simply cannot survive without affection. In fact, they can only thrive when their parents give them what some researchers have called "extravagant" amounts of affection. The human infant's need for love and affection is even more deeply rooted than the need for food. A healthy diet of affection in infancy and toddlerhood yields lifelong benefits. A study by Duke University followed five hundred children for thirty years. The 6 percent of infants who received "extravagant" levels of affection (compared with the other groups) scored higher on every measure of life and relationship satisfaction at age thirty in comparison to infants who received "normal" or "low" levels of affection. God created each one of us to need love in order to flourish — because he is love and we are destined for him.

Wired for Love

In infancy, physical touch and affection stimulate the structures of the social brain that help your baby learn to give and receive love. Extravagant physical touch and affection stimulate the parts of a baby's brain responsible for helping him become a communicative, empathetic, caring person and attentive learner. From a biological standpoint, there is simply no such thing as spoiling a baby with too much affection or attention. The more babies can be in close proximity to their parents — and especially Mom — the better it is for their overall well-being and development.

Another example of how babies are biologically wired for connection is the fact that newborns can only see for a distance of about eight to fifteen inches — roughly the distance from their mom's breast to her face. Everything beyond that distance is a scary, blurry blob. When you nurse your baby, or hold your baby close — especially when you make eye-to-eye, skin-to-skin contact with your baby — you are creating a deep, biological, psychological, relational connection between you and your baby. The cascade of calming hormones that are released in both a mom's and a baby's body during nursing and/or skin-to-skin contact produce warm feelings that facilitate the deep bonding that's essential for the well-being of mother and infant.

Nursing

It can be surprising for some parents to discover that, in Catholic theology, there's a moral case for a mother to nurse her children *if* she is at all able to do so. As Mary Shivanandan, professor emerita of the Pontifical John Paul II Institute for Studies on Marriage and Family, notes:

> The teaching of the Church, founded on the philosophy of Thomas Aquinas, is clear. Nursing is a natural duty of mother-hood and, therefore, in most cases, an obligation. … The obligation of maternal nursing is of the constant and received moral teaching of the Church, as based on natural law as well as the revealed law of the Decalogue in the fourth commandment on parental duties.
>
> For centuries this duty was taught, and was in the moral manuals up to relatively recent times. Pope Benedict XIV (1675–1758), who headed the Church from 1740–1758, gave a comprehensive statement of traditional teaching on the moral obligation of maternal nursing. He drew on … [many theological commentaries as well as the writings of] Saints Gregory the Great, Clement, Basil, Ambrose and John Chrysostom. The mother, indeed, is free of grave sin if she does not nurse, provided she has reasonable cause and provides a substitute, but he continues to affirm the duty of a mother to nurse her own children.

Shivanandan goes on to reference an address given by Saint John Paul to the Pontifical Academy of Sciences. He said, "The very individual and private act of a mother feeding her infant can lead us to a deep and far-ranging critical rethinking of certain social and economic presuppositions, the negative and moral consequences of which are becoming more and more difficult to ignore."

In other words, the nursing mother serves as a radically countercultural witness. Her very existence challenges the most basic assumptions the secular world makes about what's truly important and how things "should" get done. The fact that nursing is so controversial in some quarters is a powerful sign of what a countercultural, social witness nursing is. From a Catholic point of view, a nursing mother is not just feeding her child's body, she is also laying the groundwork for both her child's moral and spiritual framework and a just society!

To be abundantly clear, none of this is about shaming a mother who is unable to nurse for serious medical or psychological reasons. But it is important to know that, from the Church's point of view, the question of nursing one's child is not a simple matter of "my body, my choice." The Theology of the Body reminds us that our bodies have been given to us to work for the good of others. A mother doesn't need breastmilk for her own sake. God gives it to her in trust so she can bless her child with this truly sacred and miraculous gift. The host of benefits both babies and mothers receive from the nursing relationship can — and, in our opinion, should — be viewed as God's way of both praising the nursing mother for her heroic commitment to self-giving love and blessing the child with a food that not only conveys nourishment, but his grace. The nursing mother is truly discipling her child on every level.

Turn to Me

The good feelings that accompany nursing and skin-to-skin contact make your baby want to look at your face, mirror your expressions, and attend to your voice. Developmental psychologists tell us these actions form the basis of a child's capacity for moral reasoning. Although it might seem strange to speak of an infant's moral development, there's a lot going on here. These early skin-to-skin interactions lay a deep neurological foundation that make your child want to turn to you and listen to you. Later on, even when you're asking them to do hard things, like doing their chores or following your rules or choosing to do the right thing over the selfish thing, these early interactions lay a foundation in the deepest parts of your baby's brain that says, "In spite of myself, I *want* to listen to my parents because, on some deeper level that I can't explain, it just feels right."

At every age and stage, discipling your child means teaching them to turn to you for guidance on faithful ways to meet their needs and find happiness. It means communicating to your child — nonverbally even more than verbally — that you are the person to whom they can turn for the lessons on living a godly, fulfilling (and, coincidentally, virtuous) life. Recall the House of Discipleship.

Infancy and toddlerhood is the foundation of the House of Discipleship. It is the time of "embodied discipleship." At this stage, discipling

House of Discipleship

Stage Four: Relational Discipleship (Adolescence)

Teen turns toward parent to develop skills for having godly relationships and finding place in world.

Stage Three: Vocational Discipleship (Middle Childhood)

Child turns toward parent to discover and develop gifts in a way that helps him glorify God and make meaningful contributions to family and others.

Stage Two: Foundational Discipleship (Early Childhood)

Child turns toward parent to learn the stories, rules, and structures that lead to a love-filled, well-ordered life.

Stage One: Embodied Discipleship (Infancy and Toddlerhood)

Child turns toward parent to learn self-regulation and empathy through body-to-body communication.

your child doesn't involve verbal, conscious lessons about living virtuously. Instead, you're laying down the literal foundations of character and faith development. Think of it this way: Specific lessons aside, if you were in school, you would probably learn better in a warm, comfortable, sunny, cheerful classroom than in a cold, dark basement. The quality of the relationship you have with your child is the school building in which the lessons of discipleship are learned. Faith and morals tend to stick with a child to the degree that their relationship with their parents is warm, loving, generous, and safe. In infancy, Discipleship Parenting is about creating the warm, loving, embodied relationship with your child that makes them feel — on a physical and unconscious level — that they *want* to learn what you have to teach them, not because you have the power to force them to, but because it feels good to be in your presence and turn to you for help and guidance.

Self-Soothing

In some circles, there is a good deal of concern about helping babies become independent. While perhaps well-intentioned, this concern is utterly baseless and unscientific. Biologically, neurologically, and cognitively speaking, babies don't even have the capacity to know that they're separate beings from their moms until they are at least eight months old. A baby has no concept of "independence" for at least the first year of life. Having spent the first nine months of their life growing inside Mom, from a baby's perspective, Mom is physically part of *them*.

Of course, once they're born, babies are outside their mom's body, but having listened to Mom's breathing, heart rate, body sounds, and voice for nine months, babies still depend on all of Mom's bodily rhythms to set and reset their own. If a baby is stressed for any reason — because they're hungry, can't fall asleep, cranky because they're just waking up, frightened by something, or uncomfortable in any way — their brain hasn't developed to the point that they can get their bodies to calm down on their own. How could they? They can't talk themselves through their concerns. They don't have the basic mind-body control that allows them to consciously decide to take a "deep, cleansing breath," pace themselves, or wrap their arms around themselves to warm up. Again, they haven't even realized that they are separate beings from Mom yet. Infants cannot reset their bodies after a stressful event unless the parent's (ideally the mom's) body triggers that reset.

That's why we strongly recommend attachment parenting practices such as extended nursing on request (i.e., nursing when the baby asks for it instead of imposing a schedule, and nursing for comfort at least through toddlerhood), nighttime parenting (i.e., either practicing *safe* bedsharing with your infant, or at least having baby in the same room with you), and baby-wearing (i.e., using a baby sling or other similar wrap that keeps baby literally as close to your heart and face as possible). These practices enable your body to be on good speaking terms with your child's body. By using these types of parenting strategies — not in a grudging or dutiful way, but with a genuine desire to create a strong relationship with your child — you help your baby's body learn to calm down and feel safe, secure, and loved. This embodied sense of rightness, this feeling that "I am safe and lovable," is foundational to a healthy, holy life. It's among the greatest gifts parents could give their children.

This is also the reason we just as strongly discourage parents from letting their babies "cry it out," especially as part of a sleep training program. Though many people (even professionals) casually recommend sleep training (a.k.a. "Ferberizing"), if you ask them to justify their advice, they will be unable to describe any actual scientific process by which a baby can learn to self-soothe. There isn't a shred of empirical evidence — and there is a great deal of evidence to the contrary — to suggest that a baby is capable of self-soothing. A baby who is left to cry it out will eventually stop, but the most likely explanation is that the child is demonstrating "learned helplessness."[1] Simply put, the baby realizes that no one will come, so he gives up. Learned helplessness is a contributor to both insecure attachment and depression in childhood and adulthood. For a powerful illustration of learned helplessness, go to YouTube to watch the classic "Still Face Experiment" by Harvard psychologist Dr. Ed Tronick. The two-and-a-half-minute video shows how quickly a baby goes from bubbly and excited to depressed and disengaged when no one responds to him. The silence produced by ignoring a baby is not the silence of contentment. It's the silence of despair.

By contrast, using attachment parenting strategies like extended nursing on request, baby-wearing, and nighttime parenting (in a sincere and ungrudging way) enables you to teach your child the steps of self-control and self-regulation one breath at a time, one heartbeat at a time, until your little one's brain and body develop sufficiently to display good self-regulation.

On Sleep

But what about helping babies get through the night peacefully? According to Lori Feldman-Winter, lead researcher for the American Academy of Pediatrics Safe Sleep Task Force, "It is dangerous to put babies in another room. There is a tenfold increase risk of SIDS [Sudden Infant Death Syndrome] from solitary sleep for an entire year."[2] Again, this is due to the fact that a baby takes its physiological cues from Mom's body. Every human being stops breathing for brief periods while they sleep. After the first year of life, the brain develops sufficiently to automatically restart respiration after these brief moments of apnea, but for the first twelve months of life, physical proximity to Mom's body reminds the baby's body to start breathing again. Sleeping with your baby nearby has been shown to reduce the risk of SIDS by 50 percent in the first year of life.

Keeping your baby in your bed, in a co-sleeper, or in your room enables you to respond promptly, generously, and consistently to your infant at night. Early research on co-sleeping failed to consider whether parents were following safe co-sleeping practices. This caused various professional societies, including the AAP, to caution parents about co-sleeping. However, the latest research shows that as long as parents employ safe co-sleeping practices, co-sleeping is not only safe, but the most beneficial approach for promoting infant development.[3] According to a large-scale 2020 study of co-sleeping conducted by the University of Durham Infancy and Sleep Centre, "In the new protocol, breastfeeding mothers and babies are not advised against bedsharing, as long as no dangerous circumstances exist." Researchers defined "dangerous circumstances" as "sleeping with an adult on a sofa or armchair; sleeping next to an adult impaired by alcohol, medications, or illicit drugs; tobacco exposure; and preterm birth." They also recommend that babies should always sleep on their backs, naturally positioned away from pillows or anything that could obstruct their airways. They also found that "Breastfeeding mothers instinctively form a protective position around their baby." This latest research is consistent with several studies conducted by the Mother-Baby Behavioral Sleep Lab at the University of Notre Dame, which strongly advocates sleep-sharing and other attachment parenting practices.[4] These tips can get you started. Our book *Then Comes Baby: The Catholic Guide to Surviving and Thriving in the First Three Years of Parenthood* offers an extended discussion of safe nighttime parenting practices.

While many parents worry that they won't sleep as well with the baby nearby, research indicates that parents who practice attachment parenting strategies actually sleep better than parents who leave the baby in a separate room.[5] That's because the closer your baby is, the less noise they've got to make to get your attention if they wake up. Crying babies take longer to comfort and get back to sleep than fussy babies. A study in the journal *Pediatrics* found that, contrary to conventional wisdom, most babies do not sleep for six to eight hours until after the first twelve months.[6] The truth is, no parent of an infant sleeps well. Don't make it harder on yourself. Keep your baby as close as possible at night so that you can respond to your infant promptly — and you can get the rest you need.

For more information on nighttime parenting, we recommend *Then Comes Baby* and the popular resources that can be found at the website of the Mother-Baby Behavioral Sleep Lab at the University of Notre Dame, https://cosleeping.nd.edu.

A Point of Order

At this point we want to be clear about something. We're not suggesting that you will somehow ruin your baby if you don't use these practices. We also are not saying that you are a failure as a parent or a Catholic if you don't follow our recommendations. That said, it's absolutely true that, except in cases where there is a serious medical or psychiatric need to do so (e.g., medical complications with nursing or severe postpartum depression) it is, frankly, difficult to justify other, less body-based, conventional parenting practices (such as bottle-feeding, sleeping separately from your infant, or extensive use of devices that create physical separation between parents and infants) as appropriate from a Catholic perspective. Attachment parenting practices are much more consistent with the Catholic insight that joy is tied to self-giving, and that God has given us our bodies to share his self-giving love with others.

Likewise, as child development expert Margot Sunderland illustrates in her book, *The Science of Parenting*, the attachment parenting practices we recommend above are unquestionably more physiologically attuned to the needs of the infant brain and body. The more we study the physical nature of the parent-child bond, the more we see that babies were created to be parented with attachment in mind.

Theologically and scientifically speaking, there is a very strong case to be made that attachment parenting practices are spiritually and biologically superior in every way. Moreover, there isn't a single study that suggests that — regardless of your parenting style — the incorporation of at least some of the attachment parenting practices we're recommending cannot make the parent-child bond stronger, the parent happier, and the child healthier. The science is clear. A little employment of attachment parenting techniques is good, and more is better — as long as it is not done grudgingly.

That said, while it's important to respond promptly, generously, and consistently to your child's cries, you are not "wrecking" your child if your baby is crying in her car seat on a short trip to the grocery store, or those times when no one is available to attend to your baby and you have to get a shower. Out of simple compassion, parents should do all they can to limit the amount of time a baby has to cry to get their attention; but despite your best efforts, your baby will sometimes cry — sometimes a lot. But sometimes, despite your best efforts, there won't be anything you can do about it. It's OK. Remember the rule we suggested earlier in the book. It's important to take the advice we offer seriously — but not scrupulously.

Our recommendation to respond to your infant's needs promptly, generously, and consistently and to limit your baby's need to cry as much as is reasonably possibly is simply intended to help you open your heart to your baby and resist common advice to be dismissive of your infant's cries. It's *not* meant to be a test that you live in constant fear of failing. Love your child. Do your honest, prayful best to respond promptly, generously, and consistently to your child. But don't do it out of fear or a desire to prove yourself. Do it so that you can fall in love with them and they can fall in love with you. Leave the rest to God's grace.

We discuss the ins and outs of practices like extended nursing on request, nighttime parenting, skin-to-skin contact, and baby-wearing in our book *Then Comes Baby: The Catholic Guide to Surviving and Thriving in the First Three Years of Parenthood*. In *Then Comes Baby*, we also discuss how to use these practices in a manner that still allows you to take care of yourself and your marriage. If you would like to learn more about the healthiest, best, and most balanced ways to use attachment parenting practices without burning out, we recommend the discussions in that title. For the purposes of *Parenting Your Kids with Grace*, it's enough to know that discipling your child in living a healthy, happy, holy life doesn't just start with the verbal lessons you teach them later in life. It starts with the body-to-body relationship that sensitive, faithful moms and dads cultivate with their infants; a relationship that says, "turn to me with your most basic questions about what it means to feel safe, loved, and good. I want to help you know your dignity and worth as a child of God in the deepest parts of your heart and mind."

Make It Fun

Above all, even though parenting a baby is hard work, do your best to have fun with your child. Research shows that play creates "neural synchrony" between parents and their baby. Play becomes a kind of communication. According to the study, researchers were surprised to find:

> The infant brain was often "leading" the adult brain by a few seconds, suggesting that babies do not just passively receive input but may guide adults toward the next thing they're going to focus on: which toy to pick up, which words to say. While communicating, the adult and child seem to form a feedback loop. The adult's brain seemed to predict when the infants would smile, the infants' brains anticipated when the adult would use more "baby talk," and both brains tracked joint eye contact and joint attention to toys. So, when a baby and adult play together, their brains influence each other in dynamic ways.[7]

This neural synchrony doesn't just exist when parents play with their infants. It exists any time parents adopt a joyful, engaging attitude toward anything they do with their children. In a sense, it is the conscious effort the parent makes to cultivate a sense of joy of being in the baby's presence that facilitates the neurological processes involved in establishing secure attachment. This also reinforces why doing attachment parenting techniques in a grudging, dutiful way does not tend to produce good results. Adopting the attitude that "I *have* to nurse" or "I *have* to co-sleep" or "I *have* to keep the baby close" (or else I will ruin my child/fail the mothering test) not only destroys your joy, but it also undoes the secure attachment you are trying to create. Remember, Baby is trying to sync his body rhythms to yours. The more stressed you are, the more your body is sending stress signals to your baby. By all means, be generous in meeting your baby's needs, but make sure to (1) expect support from the people you love, (2) attend to your health and well-being, and (3) give yourself permission to enjoy your baby.

Take time every day to read to your baby. Sing to your baby. Just enjoy cuddling with your baby. Be silly and play with your baby. Use exaggerated faces and tones when interacting with your baby. Focusing on making your baby smile when you interact with him throughout the day is just as important as feeding and changing and bathing your baby. It's good for you, too. Let your baby teach you what a gift life is. Parenting is hard work, but smiling at your child (even when you aren't feeling it) and getting them to smile back stimulates your brain with hormones that help you feel warm, connected, calm, and happy. Your baby doesn't want to just "take" from you. God designed your baby to be able to give joy back to you if you'll let him.

We know there is a lot to do, and sometimes parents of infants can feel very torn between keeping up the house and tending to the baby. Don't be afraid to ask — no, *expect* — the people who say they love you (your spouse, family, and friends) to help you. In those times when you just need to get things done, pop your baby in your sling and do what you need to do. Dads can do this too. You'll feel like superheroes when you're able to accomplish the things you need to do and keep Baby happy at the same time, because even when you're busy, your body is still saying, "Mommy/Daddy's here. You are good and loved and safe in my arms."

Hey, Dad, We're Talking to You, Too

Although we have tailored most of this chapter to moms, readers shouldn't get the impression that dads are somehow an unimportant part of the infant care picture. Despite the messages that our popular culture often gives that fathers are either incompetent or superfluous, Catholic dads should expect themselves to be the primary support for Mom and, after Mom, the person most involved in the baby's day-to-day care and nurturing. Every day, pray that God would help you be the husband and father that your wife and baby need you to be and that God is asking you to become. Ask for Saint Joseph's intercession and step into the breach!

Most importantly, dads must truly honor the hard work involved in cultivating the kind of body-to-body discipleship relationship with your child that we've been describing here. Make sure Mom has the time she needs to shower, dress, and make herself feel like a human being every day. *Cheerfully* do everything you can to take the lead in keeping up the house and getting healthy meals to the table. You can handle these tasks yourself or by finding Mom the alternative help she needs to get these things done. Just don't put it on her. Becoming a servant-leader means caring for your wife as well as she is caring for your infant. Being a nurturing mom is physically exhausting work. She doesn't need you to "pitch in." She needs you to take the lead in caring for her and doing what you can to provide an orderly, clean, pleasant, nourishing environment for her and your baby.

Although hormones do play a significant role, an equally significant factor in predicting postpartum depression is poor spousal support.[8] Your wife deserves to be able to count on you to not pressure her to "put down that baby and take care of me and the house already." Give your wife the generous care, love, and support she deserves for taking on the heroic, exhausting task of teaching your baby that he is loved, safe, and good.

Of course, your baby needs you, too. Hold your baby. A lot. If Mom needs to be busy with something and your baby is awake, your child should be in your arms. Moms don't have secret meetings where they learn to make babies happy. They learn as they go by putting in the time to learn their baby's cues and discovering their own unique strategies for comforting their little one. You'll learn your own strategies if you're willing to put in the time too. Don't hand the baby off to Mom as soon as the baby starts fussing. Take a few minutes to work it out.

Involved fathers bring lots of unique gifts to the parenting table. Involved dads help babies learn to speak sooner and use more words because they use less baby talk than moms do. Baby talk helps infants learn how to form words, but more mature communication helps babies learn sentence structure and vocabulary. Other studies suggest that while Mom's presence stimulates the part of the infant's brain that helps babies cope with stress, Dad's presence helps infants learn to manage aggression and frustration.

By all means, play with your baby, but do it gently. Be careful to not roughhouse with an infant. Baby should never be shaken or jerked around, as this can cause serious damage to their still-developing brain. Although moms can nurse, there are still lots of ways dads can use the unique body God has given them to love their infant. Tickle baby's neck or tummy with your five o'clock shadow. Talk and sing to your baby with your deeper voice. Hold your baby to your chest and help baby discover that there are other "songs" to learn besides the "music" of his mommy's heart and body. Dad, as "first other," plays a big part in helping Baby feel that he can continue to feel good, loved, and safe as he enters the world.

Finally, Catholic dads should cheerfully play an active role in bathing, changing, and attending to the other physical needs of your baby. Even when Mom is taking point on these activities, you should be right next to her doing them with her as much as possible. Adopting this attitude helps Mom feel supported and helps your baby see you as an integral part of the team. That will make switching off baby care when Mom needs a break that much easier.

For more ideas on how dads can become fathers after the Father's own heart, check out Dr. Greg's book, *The BeDADitudes: Eight Ways to Be an Awesome Dad*, as well as the fathering sections in *Then Comes Baby*.

What About Working Moms?

Times are such that most moms must return to work sometime after their children are born. In the past, some readers have assumed that the approach we advocate is only for stay-at-home moms. That simply isn't true. In fact, when both parents work outside the home, it is even more important to use the strategies we've discussed in this chapter so that Mom, Dad, and Baby can develop the closest relationship possible despite having to spend time apart during the day.

First, do look into the option of working remotely. Virtual offices are becoming much more common. With a little creativity and persistence, these arrangements can allow many parents to experience the best of both worlds.

If working remotely isn't an option, do your best to arrange for the same person to care for your child personally every day. Try to avoid group day care environments as much as possible; but if you need to use a group day care, choose one that has the highest caregiver-to-child ratio.

When you're home, wear your baby in a sling or similar wrap that allows close, body-to-body contact with your child. Nurse your child for as long as you are able, pumping breastmilk for feedings during the time you have to be away from your child. If you bottle-feed, try to make the experience as close to nursing as possible. Always hold the bottle close to your body. You might even wish to place your baby against your breast while you bottle-feed so that your baby can hear your heart sounds and smell you. As much as possible, use the same blanket to feed your baby every day and ask your caregiver to hold your baby in it when they feed him or her. The familiar feelings and scent of you will provide extra comfort in those times you can't be there (but, by all means, wash the blanket as necessary). You might even wish to use your phone to make a recording of you cooing and singing to your baby and ask your caregiver to play the audio file so your child can hear your voice when they are feeding your baby. Be creative about finding ways to "be there" even when you can't be there.

When you are home, make evenings about being a family. As long as you feel safe doing so, keep your baby close in the sling as you do chores and meal prep. Create a regular rhythm to your evenings — for your sake as well as the baby's.

Finally, we believe that nighttime parenting (i.e., co-sleeping) is especially important when both parents must be away from baby during the day. Remember, infancy is all about body-to-body communication.

Sleep time isn't down time for baby. Your infant is still relating to you and learning to set his bodily rhythms even when he is sleeping. Sleeping close to your baby facilitates the first physiological lessons of self-regulation.

Wrapping Up

Discipleship Parenting in infancy is first about learning to be still and receive the love God has for you so you can share it with your little one and let that love sink down deep into your baby's very biology. Every day, through a million little efforts to respond promptly, generously, and consistently to your baby's needs, you're helping them learn that being loved and learning how to love someone back is a good, safe, and godly thing to do. This is the most important lesson a human being can learn. It's the foundation of the Great Commandment: to love one another as God has loved us.

Some days will be harder than others. That's why it's important to make it a priority to get whatever help is necessary to make sure that your needs are being met. You need to feel at least basically clean, nourished, healthy, and sane. You can't give your baby a sense that he is being well cared for if you aren't being well cared for yourself.

Finally, give yourself permission to enjoy the process. Sometimes you'll be exhausted. Sometimes you'll feel like crying yourself. Sometimes you'll wonder whether you've gotten in over your head. Just remember that all of that is normal. You're doing the best you can. God is parenting with you. The whole point is to let God crack open your heart so that you can learn to give and receive his love a little better.

Prayer

Lord, as I hold my baby in my arms, let me feel your arms wrapped around me. As my baby rests in my embrace, help me to be still and know that you are my God. When my own stores run dry, fill me up with your love, patience, peace, and energy. Come into my heart in a deeper way and let me love my child as generously as you love me.

Holy Family, pray for us. Amen.

Discussion Questions

How is God using your relationship with your baby to help you draw closer to him?

What ideas in this chapter were the most helpful to you as a parent of an infant? Which do you find most challenging?

You don't have to do it alone. Every parent needs help. What needs are you having a hard time meeting as you attend to your infant? What can you do to let the people in your life (especially your spouse) know that you need help meeting these needs?

CHAPTER 24

Discipling Your Toddler (Twelve to Thirty-Six Months)

See that you do not despise one of these little ones,
for I say to you that their angels in heaven always
look upon the face of my heavenly Father.

Matthew 18:10

People talk a lot about the terrible two's. It can be easy to become frustrated with toddlers. For the first thirty-six months, infants and toddlers are still working to learn the basics of bodily and emotional control. They are, literally, taking their first steps toward autonomy, the ability to understand themselves as independent beings. But that's a lot to work out. Because of this, toddlers are wiggly and emotional, impulsive and short-fused, independent and needy, adventurous and terrified all at the same time. It can be helpful to remember that the only thing more challenging than parenting a toddler ... is being one.

In some ways — if you'll forgive the slightly dramatic metaphor — being a toddler is like being a stroke victim. Imagine having had a stroke and trying to regain your ability to do basic tasks: walking, feeding your-

195

self, and all the rest. Imagine being able to *see* yourself doing all of these things with perfect competence but not being able to get your body to cooperate, no matter how hard you tried. Think of how stressful that would be. How often would you be tempted to give in to tears and tantrums?

Toddlerhood is very much like this. Toddlers' brains have developed to the point that they can see themselves doing almost everything perfectly. They see a piano and imagine playing every song they've heard perfectly. They see a ball and imagine being a professional ball player. They see you cooking and imagine being master chefs. They just can't make their bodies DO any of it. It. Is. Just. So. FRUSTRATING! Without Mom and Dad's help to get their emotional temperatures down, toddlers *live* at a 7.5 on the emotional temperature scale — almost always one frustration shy of a complete meltdown. The more you work with this reality instead of resenting it, the happier and more successful a parent of a toddler you will be.

Mobile Babies

Toddlers are not mini-adults with poor self-control, a bad attitude, and a willful spirit. Neurologically speaking, toddlers are just mobile babies. Like infants, they are almost completely incapable of effective self-regulation. Toddlers almost constantly need to be at the side of or in the arms of their moms and dads in order to keep their emotional temperatures low enough to learn everything they need to know to graduate to early childhood as emotionally calm, behaviorally focused, intellectually attentive persons.

The main tasks for Discipleship Parents in toddlerhood are helping toddlers learn the basics of emotional regulation, bodily/behavioral control, and intellectual focus. These skills enable toddlers to enter early childhood well-prepared for more formal learning (both school and life lessons). Most parents aren't aware that these skills have to be taught. We just expect these things to happen, and punish toddlers for failing to live up to our (developmentally inappropriate) expectations. By contrast, Discipleship Parents do their best to respect God's design of their children's minds so that they can help their kids acquire these skills.

Our book *Then Comes Baby* offers an extensive look at questions related to toddlerhood, such as extended nursing and weaning, toilet training, transitioning the child to more independent sleeping arrangements, and other issues. For the sake of our discussion here, we'll focus on more general suggestions parents must keep in mind to successfully disciple their children in learning the lessons of basic self-regulation, bodily/behavioral control, and intellectual focus.

Extended Nursing

If it is at all possible, the single most important practice a mother can employ for both maintaining her own sanity and helping her toddler achieve all the milestones we listed above is *extended nursing*. Contrary to what your friends or your mother-in-law might say, it is not weird to nurse a toddler. According to the American Academy of Pediatrics, "There is no upper limit to the duration of breastfeeding and no evidence of psychologic or developmental harm from breastfeeding into the third year of life or longer."[1] Worldwide, children are commonly nursed for four years or longer.[2] Most child development experts recommend continuing to nurse your child as long as you are both happy to do so; and, as you will see in the next chapter, Scripture and Catholic tradition tend to assume children will continue to nurse to some degree until age three.

Of course, your nursing relationship will evolve as your child nurses less for nourishment and more for emotional comfort, but toddlers still receive important brain-growing benefits from breastfeeding.[3] Breastmilk is intelligent food. It changes with your child's needs. For instance, when a woman is tandem nursing an infant and a toddler, the milk she produces for her infant is different from the milk she produces for her toddler.[4] Beyond this, the peaceful spirit the nursing relationship fosters in toddlers (and Mom!) is something no parent should do without.

Many adults are oddly dismissive of the toddler's need to nurse for comfort. Comfort (i.e., self-regulation) is not just a psychological process, but also a brain-based one. As we've noted, toddlers are wiggly, impulsive, mobile infants who are incapable of getting themselves under control. There are few more effective ways of calming an overwrought, overstimulated, bouncing-off-the-walls toddler than to bring them to your breast and let them enjoy the body-regulating effect of your skin, heartbeat, and slower respiration — not to mention the wash of calming hormones that nursing provides. Nursing is tremendously helpful to Mom's sanity as well. Again, unless you are nursing, there are very few effective ways to get a toddler to be still and quiet. Extended nursing isn't technically necessary for the physical survival of your toddler; but frankly, in light of all the benefits it affords both mother and toddler (developmentally, emotionally, and relationally), it's foolish not to do it if you are at all able.

What If I Can't Nurse?

Parents who are unable to nurse can achieve similar benefits by practicing a nursing-based approach to bottle-feeding. When your toddler needs a little extra TLC or help re-regulating, fill a bottle with toddler formula and hold him close to your breast as he drinks so that he can gain the extra-comforting benefit of body-to-body contact. Many adoptive parents — ourselves included — have found this approach to bottle-feeding critical for fostering strong attachment. Never let your toddler wander around with a bottle. Discipleship Parents should take advantage of every opportunity to teach their children to see them as the source of all the good things they need to thrive.

Again, *Then Comes Baby* offers a larger discussion of these questions. We invite interested readers to turn to that resource for additional support.

Nighttime Parenting

Continuing some version of nighttime parenting (i.e., keeping the toddler in bed, in a co-sleeper, or in your room) is also an important way to facilitate the toddler's ability to achieve emotional regulation, bodily/behavioral control, and intellectual focus. The toddler brain continues to process stress all night long. Trying to get back to sleep after waking or having a nightmare is very stressful. According to the National Sleep Foundation, 68 percent of *adults* struggle with falling and staying asleep. Just imagine how difficult it can be for toddlers, whose capacity for self-regulation is still developing.

Many parents who transition older infants into separate rooms are surprised when their toddler starts clamoring to return to their mom and dad's bed. This is not a manipulative ploy for attention. As your toddler's brain develops, their visual perception and imagination grow by leaps and bounds. A newborn can only see six inches in front of his face. A toddler can see the whole room — along with all the shadows and spooky-looking things that seem to fill it at night. Toddlers are also more aware that they are separate beings from Mom, so they are more aware of their vulnerability. All of this adds up to a toddler's increased ability to scare himself senseless at night. Because toddlers are still developing their brain-based capacity for self-regulation, they don't just need Mom and Dad's comfort for emotional reasons. They need to be physically close to Mom and/or Dad to get their revved-up bodies and brains back under control and have a peaceful night's sleep.

A Word About Sleep Training

Toddlerhood is the time when many parents attempt sleep training or "Ferberizing." We would discourage this. As we discussed in the chapter on infancy, there are good reasons to believe that the conventional approach to sleep training — in which parents (to varying degrees) ignore their toddler's cries until the child falls back to sleep — is not best for developing your child's capacity for self-regulation. Research suggests that sleep training practices produce elevated levels of the stress hormone cortisol in the child's brain.[5] We know that prolonged exposure to cortisol in the brain tends to affect the brain's ability to process stress and fear. It can also lead to an increased likelihood of future behavioral health problems.[6] While sleep training does not automatically cause mental health issues down the road,[7] infants and toddlers left to cry are 200 percent more likely to exhibit behavior problems, hyperactivity, mood problems, and pathological levels of defiance by age six as infants and toddlers whose daytime and nighttime needs are met promptly, generously, and consistently.[8]

Discipleship Parents should encourage their toddlers to turn to them for help with their nighttime struggles. Let your toddler stay with you in your room in whatever arrangement works best. At the very least, stay with your toddler in his room until he falls back to sleep. We recognize that this is a tough issue to navigate. *Then Comes Baby* offers additional resources and ideas for helping you get your toddler through the night without losing your mind.

Reading

Having daily story time is also a great way to help toddlers learn to be still and quiet. It also fosters the development of your toddler's attention and verbal skills. For parents who practice extended nursing, pairing nursing with reading time is a wonderful way to establish a foundation for a lifelong love of learning in general. We can't think of a better way to instill a passion for reading than to condition your child to associate books with the warmth of your skin against his cheek and your smiling, expressive eyes reflected in his gaze.

Some parents mistakenly assume that since toddlers can't speak well, they shouldn't start reading to their children until early childhood; but there are a host of benefits to reading to your toddler. The journal *Pediatrics* found that toddlers who are read to are significantly less hyperactive and have better self-control and social skills by early childhood than toddlers whose parents did not read to them.[9] They are also much better positioned for early school success (both behaviorally and academically).

Religious parents can gain an extra benefit from reading time by mixing in a generous number of picture books about Bible stories and lives of the saints. We can't think of a better foundation for your child's faith development than letting your toddler cuddle up in your lap while nursing and reading a picture book about how much Jesus loves them. For more ideas on fostering toddler faith development, check out our book *Discovering God Together: The Catholic Guide to Raising Faithful Kids.*

Toddler Accompaniment

Because toddlers don't always want to be held, carried, or seated on their parents' laps, many parents make the mistake of thinking they can let their toddlers occupy themselves in another room while they try to get chores or other projects done. These parents often become frustrated by having to constantly interrupt what they are doing to either attend to their toddler's cries or stop their little one from destroying something, hurting themselves, or lashing out at a baby brother or sister.

Toddlers should not be left out of your sight. They are simply too impulsive to be left alone for even a minute. This doesn't mean you can't ever do anything except sit and watch your toddler while your house falls down around you. A technique we call "toddler accompaniment" helps you get things done and still be present for your toddler.

In discipleship terms, "accompaniment" is the process by which a mentor shows their disciple how to live a godly, virtuous life. Toddler accompaniment enables you to show your toddler how to use his growing independence responsibly. Toddler accompaniment takes advantage of your child's desire to be close to you and still "help" (in their own completely unhelpful toddlery way). It teaches them to use their toddler powers for good!

Toddler accompaniment involves finding ways to help your toddler engage in productive play beside you while you get things done. For instance, instead of putting your toddler in a play pen or separate room while you are making dinner, set them up in their high chair at the kitchen table or counter and give them toy food and kitchen implements so they can "help" you make dinner. Talk to them while you're working. Tell them what you're making. Ask them what they're cooking. Make a game of "tasting" the delicious dishes they are preparing.

Do you need to dust or vacuum? Don't send them away. Give them a clean dustrag and a toy vacuum and have them follow you around. It's OK if they get distracted from their "chore." If they start wandering too far or getting into something they shouldn't, just cheerfully prompt them that you still need their "help" and praise them for what a good job they're doing.

Need to fold laundry? Have your toddler hand you socks from the hamper. Be playful about it. Don't view chores as things you have to get through. See them as bonding opportunities. As your toddler gets older, you can even use these sorts of activities to teach colors and shapes. "This is a blue sock! Can you help me find another blue sock?"

These are just a few examples. With a little creativity, you can keep your toddler safe, close, and engaged even while you get household and other work done. Plus, it's never too early to encourage self-donation. There should never be a time in your children's lives when they aren't expected to do even the little bit they can to contribute to a more peaceful household. Toddler accompaniment makes helpfulness second nature to your kids. It also models the idea that chores aren't just about getting things done; they can also be an important way to build connection with others and even have fun — as long as you do them in a way that lets you "choose the better part" and prioritize relationship over simple productivity (see Lk 10:42).

Hold Hands or Hold You

The Hold Hands or Hold You Rule we discussed in the discipline section is another example of toddler accompaniment. Toddlers are still learning to be good stewards of the gift of mobility. They need your help to explore the world responsibly. When you leave the house, your toddler should be either holding your hand or, if they resist, held in your arms. This simple practice helps stop you from becoming the parent who's always complaining about your toddler constantly getting into things and how you can't look away for even a minute. The Hold Hands or Hold You Rule gives parents peace of mind by teaching your toddler to stay tethered to you — relationally as well as physically.

Toddler Discipline

It is not uncommon for parents to speak of "willful" and "disobedient" toddlers. While toddlers naturally struggle with listening or sticking with anything more than a few minutes (the average attention span at fifteen to twenty months is two to three minutes; twenty to twenty-four months is three to five minutes; twenty-five to thirty-six months is as long as six to seven minutes), toddler misbehavior is not caused so much by willfulness as it is by dysregulation. As we have noted repeatedly, a toddler's thinking brain is just starting to come online. Everything feels new, and toddlers are very easily overstimulated. Add to this our point that toddlers feel like stroke victims, and it is easy to see why toddlers are almost always at a six or seven on the emotional temperature scale. The more you focus on *preventive* approaches to helping your toddler keep her emotional temperature low, the better behaved your toddler will be.

Toddler discipline focuses on almost constant collecting, time-in, and redirecting. If you want a toddler to stop doing something, don't waste time yelling or punishing them. Simply give them something else to do. A toddler's brain gets very easily locked on a target. If you just say, "Don't do that," and fail to redirect them to another activity, their brain will force them to reengage in the activity you just told them not to do —

over and over again. Toddlers struggle to self-redirect. Redirecting them to another activity captures their focus and attention and allows them to leave behind an undesirable activity with less fuss. The key to making this work is having a pleasant, excited tone of voice that says your alternative suggestion is SO MUCH MORE FUN than the undesirable thing they were doing.

If they push back, collect them to help them calm down. Then, give them a choice of two (no more) alternative activities and require them to choose one. Be firm but maintain that pleasant, excited tone. They cannot do *that* thing, but they can choose one of these two super-awesome things you'd prefer them to do!

Don't ever argue or negotiate with a terrorist — um, that is, *toddler.* If you need them to move and they refuse, don't say another word. Gently and calmly pick them up and move them. Toddler won't get in the tub? Don't argue. Say in a pleasant, sympathetic tone, "Oh my, somebody doesn't want a bath today!" Then pick them up, give them a big kiss or a little tickle, and put them in the tub. Toddler won't pick up a toy? Use that same pleasant, sympathetic tone to say, "Goodness, it IS hard to put things away sometimes. We can do it together." Then gently put the toy in their hand, walk them to the toy box, and deposit the toy. Don't ever try to convince a toddler to cooperate. Gently — but with empathy and good humor — show them with your actions (not words) that disobeying you is simply not an option.

Keep 'em Close

Of course, the best place for a misbehaving toddler to be is in your arms or worn on your hip in a sling (which can be safely used up to forty-five pounds). A fussy toddler is fussy because she is dysregulated. She won't be able to take down her emotional temperature until she can sync up to your (calmer) body. Keeping your fussy or misbehaving toddler close is the quickest way to make this happen.

As we mentioned in the discipline chapter, please do not ever attempt a time-out with a toddler. Time-outs simply don't work at this stage. Time-outs require children to be able to calm themselves down, think through the consequences of their actions, and brainstorm alternative ideas. Toddlers can't do any of these things. Time-outs shouldn't be used before age five or six at the earliest, and even then, used sparing-ly. By contrast, collecting your toddler and getting time-in by nursing, cuddling, carrying, or "wearing" him close to your body in some way helps your child learn to see you as the person who can always help him find his peaceful place.

If Your Toddler Escalates

You may find that trying to collect or hold your toddler results in them tantrumming even harder. This usually happens because the toddler is at a 9 or higher on their emotional temperature scale. At this temperature, the child is so dysregulated that everything you do may make things worse — at first. Take a breath. You're doing fine. As long as you can keep *your* cool, the best thing to do is to hold your little one close to your chest with your arms wrapped snugly around their arms so they can't hit you, their head tucked under your chin so they can't headbutt you, and their legs wrapped around your sides so they can't kick you. In this position, the toddler is essentially immobilized, wrapped in your loving arms and held as close to you as possible. They will escalate, but keep talking softly and encouragingly. Rub their back. Get a cool cloth for their hot, sweaty head. Take deep breaths and ask them to breathe with you. Eventually they will exhaust themselves. The storm will pass, and they will melt into you. As they calm down, see whether you can get them to nurse a bit. Read a story. Help them regain their composure and their connection to you. It may take fifteen minutes or more to work through this process if your child is at the top end of the temperature scale, but it is worth the investment. The only alternative is going to war with your toddler, esca-lating the tension in your house until you both collapse exhausted, an-gry, and burned out. Who needs that? True, the preventive approach ad-vocated by Discipleship Parenting requires a little more thoughtfulness on the front end, but it pays huge dividends.

"No, Thank You"

Toddlers make a full-time job out of saying "No!" Show your little dis-ciple how to wield this power respectfully. When you need to say no to your toddler, say, "No, thank you!" instead. It may seem odd to do this with a toddler who is reaching for an electrical outlet, or pulling on the tablecloth, or any number of things that they shouldn't be doing, but if you say it frequently enough, your toddler will come to think of "NoThankYou" as one word.

It makes a huge difference when you have to take your toddler out of church or a store or playdate if they are screaming, *"NoThankYou! NoThankYou! NoThankYou!* rather than if they are wailing *"NOOOOOOOOOOOOOOOOOOO!"* The first is kind of adorable and will get you a ton of sympathy from all the adults around you, who are amazed that your child is so polite even when they're melting down. The second, not so much. The "No, thank you" technique is an important — and lifesaving — first lesson in good manners.

Teaching "Gentle"

Toddlers are great at whapping things — people, pets, you name it. They really don't mean to. They don't have the small-motor coordination required to be consistently gentle. You have to teach them. When your toddler casually hits or whaps someone or something, calmly take their hand and help them touch the person, pet, or thing gently while saying, "Let's be *gen-tle. Gen-n-n-tle.*" Taking their hand and demonstrating gentleness helps them develop the small-motor coordination to do it more efficiently. Pairing the word with this action helps them learn to respond to your verbal prompt.

Sign Language

Toddlers struggle to communicate verbally. It can be helpful to teach your toddler basic sign language for words like "please," "thank you," "I love you," and other simple words or phrases. Say the word and use the sign when talking with your toddler. Then, gently take their hand and show them how to make the motion. For instance, the sign for "please" is placing your palm on your chest and moving it in a clockwise circle. Before giving something to your child, hold it in front of them and move their hand through the motion while saying, "Please." Then praise them and give them the toy or treat. Eventually, they will learn to ask nicely for things instead of pointing and yelling. Teach other signs using a similar process. The internet is full of ideas for building a simple ASL vocabulary.

Lead Them Not into Temptation

One of the most important practices in discipleship discipline for toddlers is "leading them not into temptation." It's hard enough to be a toddler without having to negotiate all the breakable knicknacks, little projects, and booby traps that Mom, Dad, and siblings keep leaving out. Toddler-proof everything. Keep anything you don't want them to touch out of reach. Let older children know where they can keep projects and special toys so that their toddler brother or sister can't get to them.

Occasionally parents object to this, saying that the child should learn to accommodate them, not the other way around. Christian parents who pray the Our Father have no business claiming this. We can hardly ask God to "lead us not into temptation" if we're constantly setting up our own toddlers to fail. Parenting provides us opportunities to practice extending the mercy to our children that we would like to receive from God. Making a generous effort to toddler-proof your home is a good way to start.

Toileting

Finally, a brief word about toilet training. *Then Comes Baby* walks readers through all the steps they need to accomplish this, but here are a few simple things to keep in mind.

First, toileting is not a discipline issue. It is a developmental issue. You will be working against yourself (and your child) if you try to force it. It takes time for your toddler to build the neurological network that links his thinking brain to muscles that control his bowels. It takes even longer to develop the neurological network that allows your toddler to do this consciously and at will.

Second, because of all this, it's going to take longer than you think — even much longer — to potty train your child. On average, most children learn to maintain daytime continence by about three years old and nighttime continence by about four. Many children require some degree of assistance up to age six. Be patient and understanding. This is not a test or a competition. It isn't about proving yourself to your friends in the parent group. It is about lovingly accompanying your child as he learns to control his body. Practicing a gentle, supportive approach to these early lessons will establish the discipleship dynamic that will guide you and your child through future hard-to-learn lessons.

Terrific Two's

The "two's" can actually be pretty terrific. It all comes down to your willingness to surrender your desire to force your child to meet arbitrary goals, milestones, and expectations that are not developmentally appropriate, and instead humbly listening to what your little disciple's brain and body "say" about the kind of support they need to stay regulated and develop according to the schedule God naturally built into them.

Your toddler is not a little grown-up. He is a mobile baby. Even though toddlers are eager to run and explore, they need almost as much comfort, support, and presence as they did for the first twelve months. Honoring this fact allows you to respond to your toddler's needs in a way that inclines their heart to yours and solidifies the peaceful bond that will set you both up for a successful transition to early childhood.

Prayer

Lord, as I parent my squirmy, wiggly, temperamental toddler, help me to reflect on all the ways I fight back against your love, guidance, and grace. Let me be inspired by the gentle, patient ways you deal with me so that I might be similarly gentle and patient with my little one. Teach us both to be still and focused on learning the steps of love and service.

Holy Family, pray for us. Amen.

Discussion Questions

How is God using your relationship with your toddler to help you draw closer to him?

What ideas in this chapter were the most helpful to you as a parent of a toddler? Which do you find most challenging?

You don't have to do it alone. Every parent needs help. What needs are you having a hard time meeting as you attend to your toddler? What can you do to let the people in your life (especially your spouse) know that you need help meeting these needs?

CHAPTER 25

Discipling Your Three- to Six-Year-Old with Grace

I have stilled my soul, Like a weaned child to its mother,
weaned is my soul. Israel, hope in the LORD, now and forever.

Psalm 131:2–3

In his reflection on the above quote from Psalm 131, Pope Benedict XVI beautifully illustrates God's plan for your child's transition from toddlerhood into early childhood:

> Thus, we move on to the unforgettable image of the mother and child. The original Hebrew text does not speak of a newborn child but of a child that has been "weaned" (Ps 131[130]:2). Now, it is known that in the ancient Near East a special celebration marked the official weaning of a child, usually at about the age of three (cf. Gn 21:8; 1 Sm 1:20-23; 2 Mc 7:27).

The child to which the Psalmist refers is now bound to the mother by a most personal and intimate bond, hence, not merely by physical contact and the need for food. It is a more conscious tie, although nonetheless immediate and spontaneous. This is the ideal parable of the true "childhood" of the spirit that does not abandon itself to God blindly and automatically, but serenely and responsibly.

Seen through a modern lens, we tend to think of a "weaned child" as a kid who has (finally!) achieved some independence and is giving Mom a well-earned break. But as Pope Benedict XVI's reflection shows, that isn't what the psalmist means at all. The "weaned child" of the psalm would have been at least three years old. He is no longer a toddler. Until now, he has seen himself and Mommy as a unit. Having received the nurturing and support he needed to discover his autonomy, he is now a child who is developmentally ready to leave the infant years behind (including the "mobile baby" years of toddlerhood) and begin taking his first steps into early childhood. Through their extended nursing relationship, the mother of the weaned child has created an intimate, body-to-body, heart-to-heart bond. Through her inspiring commitment to self-giving love, the mother's child has learned to be still at her feet, to rest in her love, and to attend to her word. Through her loving attention — carrying him, nursing him, sleeping close to him, and responding to his cries (promptly, generously, and consistently) — she has tethered her little disciple's heart to hers. He has learned to listen to her not out of fear, but love. The weaned child of the psalm graduates from toddlerhood and enters into early childhood projecting an attitude that says, *My mommy has given me so many good things. She has taught me to feel safe and loved. To quiet my body and my mind when I'm sad or scared. And where to turn when I have questions or feel confused or overwhelmed. I can't wait to receive all the other good things she has to give me and teach me!*

Discipling Your Three- to Six-Year-Old

Of course, attachment and discipleship don't end with the toddler years. We continue to develop attachment by responding promptly, generously, and consistently to the needs and questions our little disciples present at every stage. For the three- to six-year-old child, this includes challenges like:

- Does "Y" **always** happen if I do "X"?
- How can I have a healthy relationship with my feelings?
- How can I develop my imagination and creativity?

House of Discipleship

Stage Four: Relational Discipleship (Adolescence)

Teen turns toward parent to develop skills for having godly relationships and finding place in world.

Stage Three: Vocational Discipleship (Middle Childhood)

Child turns toward parent to discover and develop gifts in a way that helps him glorify God and make meaningful contributions to family and others.

Stage Two: Foundational Discipleship (Early Childhood)

Child turns toward parent to learn the stories, rules, and structures that lead to a love-filled, well-ordered life.

Stage One: Embodied Discipleship (Infancy and Toddlerhood)

Child turns toward parent to learn self-regulation and empathy through body-to-body communication.

- What part do I play in this family?
- What rules does the world around me follow, and how can I understand them?

Helping your child answer these questions enables them to take the first steps toward developing a greater capacity for emotional control and moral reasoning, as well as the beginnings of a coherent value system and a heart for self-giving love. Each of these tasks is part of the process of "foundational discipleship" in the House of Discipleship.

Magical Mystery Tour

Early childhood is a wonderful time in a child's life. Everything is literally a wonder to the three- to six-year-old. Their thinking brain is coming online like a giant lightbulb illuminating everything. Children this age can exhaust parents with their never-ending questions and observations. It can be tempting to lose patience or dismiss them with distracted responses. But the more promptly, generously, and consistently you answer their queries, show genuine interest in their simple insights, and display real joy in their small accomplishments, the more you reinforce their impulse to turn to you first with the more complicated questions they'll wrestle with as they grow.

Shepherding your little disciple through early childhood means both fostering their sense of wonder and helping them focus their efforts to play, explore, and make meaning of their world.

Age Three

Your three-year-old should be able to say his name and age, be able to answer simple questions with five- or six-word sentences, and start to tell stories. These stories may wander a bit (OK, a lot), but being an attentive listener helps capture your child's heart and model the attention you want from them when you share stories and important lessons.

Securely attached three-year-olds are normally very affectionate (both boys and girls). They also display a wide range of emotions. Sometimes their emotions can feel so big it's intimidating. When Mom and Dad stay calm in the face of their little one's anger, sadness, and fear, it says, "Even when you (child) can't control your emotions, I can help you feel calm and safe again." At this stage, tantrums are still not so much a challenge to your authority as they are a sign of dysregulation. Of course, you need to be clear that things like hitting or throwing are never OK, but instead of simply punishing these behaviors, help them calm down and rehearse/role-play better ways to handle future situations.

Cognitively speaking, three-year-olds can be easily confused by multi-part requests. They can handle single-part requests, such as, "OK, honey, please put on your pj's." But "Please put on your pj's, put your clothes in the hamper, and brush your teeth" can be overwhelming. Their brains still struggle with complex commands.

Age Four

Your four-year-old's imagination is starting to bloom alongside their increased language skills. While imagination can be a great resource for children, parents should be sensitive to the fact that a little one's imagination can easily intrude on reality. The four-year-old pretending to be a knight chasing a dragon one minute can be mortally convinced the next that the same dragon is coming to eat him. More and more, your child's emotional temperature will be driven by his imagination and self-talk as much as it is by actual events.

Four-year-olds do better with two- or three-part requests: "Please put on your pj's, put your clothes in the hamper, and brush your teeth." But it is still important to be patient and not confuse distractability with disobedience. If you ask your four-year-old to do something, they will be more likely to comply if you:

- make sure they can repeat it back to you,
- see them start to do it, *and*
- check in on them at reasonable intervals.

If your child loses focus by the time you check in, it's enough to gently prompt them to get back on track. Don't get caught up in what you think your child *should* be able to do. Use preventive discipline and pay attention to the level of supervision your child actually requires to stay on task. At this stage, your child's compliance depends much more on your ability to follow through than theirs.

Four-year-olds are beginning to internalize household rules and routines, remembering the way things are typically done and what is expected of them. Their ability to do this tends to depend on the consistency of your *rituals* and *routines*. If your child's schedule varies from day to day, it will take him longer to learn what the rules are — even with you constantly telling him — than it will if the rhythm of each day is similar. Routines, not words, are the best way to teach expectations and rules. Four-year-olds need to have things programmed into their muscle memory in order to remember what is expected from one day to the next.

Four-year-olds are a little more likely to begin expressing anger and other strong emotions verbally rather than physically. Even so, they are still not very good at lowering their own emotional temperatures. They may need less help from Mom and Dad to get re-regulated, but they will still need help. By all means, be clear about what constitutes acceptable ways to express feelings, but work to be a patient, calming presence in the face of their outbursts. Help your little disciple express emotions more effectively by empathetically reflecting her feelings back to her. You might say things like, "You feel SO angry right now." "I'm so sorry to see you feeling so sad." "You seem really scared right now." Don't try to tell them they shouldn't feel X. Instead, help them brainstorm things they could do to either solve the problem or take down their emotional temperature. Give them options. For instance, "You feel so sad that you have to share your toy. Would you like to play with something else while you wait, or would you like to cuddle with me for a minute?" Don't overwhelm them with choices. Unless they offer an acceptable third option themselves, make them choose one of the options you've presented.

Four-year-olds are still struggling to connect actions with consequences. This doesn't consistently happen until age seven, the "age of reason." You can help them learn by connecting the dots when you correct them. For instance, instead of shouting, "Don't run!" say, "If you run, you can fall!" They won't completely understand how the two go together at first, but pairing behaviors and consequences will help them learn faster.

Age Five
Five-year-olds are beginning to wrestle with more complicated ques-

tions, especially questions of right and wrong. A five-year-old we know once asked, "When Robin Hood robbed from the rich and gave to the poor, was that a sin or was that good?"

Speaking of Robin Hood, five-year-olds *really* love stories. Younger children view story time as entertainment and an opportunity to connect with Mom and Dad. By age five, children understand that stories also contain moral lessons about how the world does and doesn't work. At this age, daily story time is more important than ever. You can't read enough to a child. In particular, be sure to read lots of Bible stories, children's story versions of the lives of the saints, and fables that teach values and moral reasoning. Be the person who tells your child all the stories that will help him develop his conscience and worldview. If you don't, then TV, movies, and the internet will.

Age Six

At age six, most of the pieces of higher-level thinking are installed. They're just not quite hooked up yet. Six-year-olds understand that rules are important, but they still think that rules can change in the middle of a game. The arbitrariness of the rules they develop for their own games gives you a window into how random your rules still seem to them. They have a pretty clear sense that some things are bad and some things are good, but they really haven't completely figured out *why* that is. Likewise, children at this stage tend to assume that bad things done by accident carry the same moral weight as bad things done on purpose.

Some children at this age can begin to display scrupulosity. They worry about whether this thing or that could be a sin. Because they struggle to completely understand what constitutes "good" and "bad," they may think they were "bad" because they got angry, even if they handled their anger appropriately. Or they may feel guilty because they put on their pajamas *before* they brushed their teeth, when you told them to do it the other way around. The best way to respond to this confusion is to help them lower their emotional temperature with lots of *time-in*, even more affection, and explaining, as simply as possible, the difference between willful defiance and honest mistakes.

Discipleship Discipline in Early Childhood

It is tremendously important to remember that, according to Catholic moral theology, children are incapable of committing sin until at least age seven. This is because, as we have noted, children under age seven are still learning to consistently connect actions and consequences, understand what is good and what is bad, and figure why good is good and bad is bad. From ages three to six, parents are effectively building their child's conscience.

While it is always important to be firm and clear about rules and expectations, it's also important to deal gently with infractions. Your child's conscience is a delicate thing. Harsh discipline can cause it to become too sensitive and scrupulous on the one hand, or broken altogether on the other. When parents are consistently too harsh, children don't bother to develop their own capacity for moral reasoning. They just wait to be yelled at to know that they're doing something wrong. If you're *not* yelling, regardless of the reason, they assume what they're doing is just fine.

The best approach to misbehavior at this stage is to:

- Use collecting and time-in techniques to keep your child's emotional temperature low so that their brain is able to learn and apply what you want to teach.
- Patiently ask questions to understand the driving forces behind any bad behavior.
- Gently talk *together* (i.e., discuss, don't lecture) about why the choice they made was the wrong one.
- Ask leading questions (especially the virtue-based questions we discussed in the discipling tools chapter) to help them discover healthy options and why these are better responses. Again, don't lecture. Discuss.
- Work together to identify future situations in which your child will need to remember these better responses. Role-play these scenarios to help your child integrate these responses into their muscle memory.

This patient, gentle, stepwise approach provides the trellis around which your child's capacity for healthy moral reasoning can grow. Use the techniques we discussed in the discipline section to support this basic framework.

For instance, logical consequences are particularly useful at this stage of development. Remember, logical consequences are not punishments. They are simply the things you require a child to do to clean up the mess they made (literally or metaphorically) and show you that they know how to do the right thing. Logical consequences like the ones we discussed earlier in the book help children strengthen their ability to understand both *that* Y almost always follows X and *why* that is the case.

For those times when simple redirections won't do, instead of yelling, let logical consequences do the talking for you. One of the hardest things for many parents to get past is the idea that if they aren't yelling or being severe, they are somehow being poor disciplinarians. This "logic" is rooted in the mistaken belief that the best way to teach good behavior is to make a child suffer for bad behavior. In truth, the best way to teach good behavior is *to calmly teach good behavior* by communicating expectations clearly, providing the necessary support for success, and having logical consequences to connect behaviors with outcomes. It's fine to raise your voice if you need to stop your child from doing something dangerous. But in general, yelling wastes your energy and makes the child worry more about your reactions than their behavior.

It can be hard to resist the temptation to yell — and again, we don't mean to imply that yelling occasionally is some kind of grave offense against the dignity of your child. But parents who are habitual yellers would do well to practice monitoring their own emotional temperatures and remember that they will be most effective when they bring their own temperatures below a 7 (where they are not tempted to engage in either verbal or nonverbal displays of disgust or irritation). Working to keep your own emotional temperature at a 6 or lower enables your thinking brain (cortex) to identify solutions to behavior problems that help you feel effective and competent. Allowing your temperature to habitually rise above a 7 forces you to live in your emotional and reactive brain (limbic system), which will block your creativity and make you feel powerless.

Parents use yelling as an antidote to the powerlessness we feel sometimes, but it is more of a poison than a true help. The real antidote to powerlessness is not to be found in raising our voices. Rather, it is found in taking steps to calm down and self-regulate before responding to problems. No doubt there are things you naturally do to take down your emotional temperature. Make a note of them and practice them throughout the day, especially when you are getting agitated with your kids. Use these strategies to calm down first, and then address your children's misbehavior. If you need more suggestions for lowering your emotional temperature, see our book *Unworried: A Life Without Anxiety.*

Developing Initiative and Competence

Early childhood is when children begin to have the ability to make real contributions to family life. In toddlerhood, children were able to play at doing chores with you for a few minutes at a time. Now, they enjoy being able to offer real help.

That said, children are still learning how to do things, and they are still fairly easily distracted. Rather than giving children independent chores, it is good to begin teaching initiative and responsibility by having your child do chores with you. Doing simple tasks like making their bed together, picking up their toys together, and having them help you with various simple household tasks gives children a real sense of efficacy. And if you focus on the relationship instead of just the task, it allows you to bond together over normal household activities. This is where household routines become especially important. When meals happen more or less at this time, laundry is done on these days, and cleaning bedrooms is done on those days, etc., children's behavior learns to follow the "flow" of the household. They are much less apt to complain about helping than children raised in homes where chores are handled when Mom and Dad feel like it. If parents can put off chores until they feel like doing them, why can't kids? Model responsibility and stewardship to command responsibility and stewardship.

Of course, children do need time to just play — both independently and with you. But don't make the mistake of thinking that children must be kept out of the way while you do chores. To the degree that it is safe and reasonable, children get a great deal of joy out of working alongside you.

Teaching Emotional Control

Up until now, children have had very little ability to control their emotions. In early childhood, that begins to change. With their increased language skills, children in early childhood begin developing the capacity for self-talk. That's the conversation we have inside our heads that can either pour water or gas on our emotional fires. A child who has positive self-talk might feel angry or frustrated, but he hears a voice in his head that says, "Mommy and Daddy love me and want to help me make it better. I should listen." A child who has negative self-talk might fan the flames of his emotional flare-ups with a voice that says, "This isn't fair! Nobody cares! I can't do it!"

In early childhood, children still need some assistance from their mom and dad to control their emotions, but as they move into middle childhood, they will need to take more and more responsibility for handling their own feelings. In general, there are three steps to fostering good emotional control.

1. Collecting/Time-in

Emotional control begins with learning to control one's bodily reactions to a stressor. If your child is upset, angry, fearful, or even disrespectful, they are dysregulated. Instead of yelling at the child and increasing their emotional temperature, take a deep breath and have the child sit on your lap or next to you. Take ten seconds or so to tell them that you love them. Give them a kiss. Rub their back. Start the process of re-regulation.

2. Empathize

When you're upset, you probably don't like someone yelling at you or telling you, "Just calm down." Kids don't either. Just like you, they want to feel understood. Your ability to let them know that you understand how they are feeling — and that you are not afraid of or intimidated by their emotions — sends the message that feelings are not something to be feared, but something to be managed. Once your child is in your lap or in your arms, empathize with them. Say something like:

- Wow, those are really big feelings!
- I'm so sorry that you feel so angry/sad/scared/frustrated/

(other feeling words). Sometimes I feel that way too. It's really hard to feel like that, isn't it?

- Sometimes we all feel so angry that we want to hit (or break things, or yell).

3. Offer Alternatives

Empathizing with your child doesn't mean approving of the way they expressed their feelings. In the next step, help your child see that there are better ways to manage their emotional reactions. The following chart offers some examples.

When Your Child Says/Does	Respond with
I HATE YOU!	Please say, "I'm so angry!" Have them repeat. Then say, "I know you are, honey. Let's think about what you can do to feel better."
You don't love me!	Please say, "Do you love me?" Or, "Could you hold me?" Have them repeat, then give affection while reminding them that being loving and setting rules sometimes go together.
Child calls you a name	Have child apologize. Then say, "Please say, 'I feel so (insert emotion).'" Have them repeat, then ask leading questions to help them figure out what to do about it.
Rolls eyes/Makes faces at you	Please don't make faces at me. I need you to use your words. Tell me what you are thinking. I promise I will listen.

Storms away/Slams door	Have child come back. Say, "I know you are angry, but you still have to be respectful. Please say, 'Can I have some alone time to calm down.'" Have the child repeat, then say, "Yes, thank you for asking. Take some time to calm down and then we can talk about how to handle this better next time." Remind them to walk away calmly.

Most of the time, these simple redirections will be sufficient for teaching your children better ways to manage their emotions. Sometimes, especially if you have missed the early warning signs that their emotional temperatures are escalating and they are at a 9 or 10 on the emotional temperature scale, your attempts to intervene using the above steps will seem to make things worse. In these times, your child simply needs a time-out to cool down enough to be able to accept your affection and be receptive to your instruction. Use the time-out steps outlined in the discipleship discipline section.

Fostering Healthy Socialization

Meaningful socialization starts in early childhood. This is the time for playdates and preschool. That said, healthy socialization does not begin when your child gets together with other children. It begins with healthy, well-ordered relationships within the home.

We have referenced the importance of rituals and routines throughout the book, but families tend to dismiss their importance. Do so at your peril. If you haven't established regular times every day to work, play, talk, and pray together, be sure to double-down on your effort at this stage of your child's life.

Children at this stage are all about rituals and routines. Carving out *daily* time to work, play, talk, and pray as a family helps to establish a rhythm of life in your household. Doing this is critical for helping your children understand that rather than waking up and running around willy-nilly all day, a healthy, godly life has a gentle (as opposed to rigid) structure and rhythm. Sticking to that rhythm allows our hearts to be at peace. Rituals give us time to reflect so that we can assess our own well-being, check in on the health of our relationships, and open our hearts to the ways God is communicating with us throughout the day. Of course, we're not suggesting that three- to six-year-olds are experiencing all this in family rituals. But *you* will, which will also help your kids be calmer. Likewise, by establishing regular family rituals of connection and routines in your day, you help your little disciple internalize the structure that allows them to experience these benefits later on.

Peer Socialization

Creating strong family rituals for working, playing, talking, and praying together at this stage also helps families set realistic expectations for how many playdates and activities are too many. This is the stage when many families begin to become overscheduled. They sacrifice a strong and intimate family life because they believe that socialization means never saying no to a new activity. At this stage, good socialization is primarily learned by getting lots of time to participate in family rituals with Mom and Dad. When children get together with other children, they are given an opportunity to practice the lessons (good manners, emotional control, empathy, etc.) that they learned at their parents' knee. They do not, however, learn socialization from other children. Spend five minutes on a school playground, or read *Lord of the Flies*, and you'll see what we mean.

That said, assuming you have prioritized daily family time to work, play, talk, and pray together, time with peers is also very important. Here are some tips that will help you make sure the time your kids spend with other kids goes well.

1. Review Rules and Expectations Ahead of Time

Don't wait for problems to occur. Before you leave home, use the rehearsal technique to review how your child is expected to behave. (*What do we do when X happens? Do you remember?*) Don't treat this like a test. Take a helpful, supportive tone. Review solutions to specific challenges that arose on the last playdate or day out. If you anticipate any particular problems or clashes, this is the time to use the role-playing and rehearsal techniques we outlined in our discussion of discipleship discipline.

A subset of this tip: Don't expose your children to situations you know they will fail at. For instance, if you know your child can't sit still for reading time at the library, don't take them just yet. Practice having story time at home so they can learn how to behave. Failure breeds failure. Success breeds success. Before putting your child in a social situation outside the home, do your best to give your child the opportunity to practice how to behave in that situation at home. These situations don't have to be the same. They only have to require similar types of behavior. For instance, children who are helped to stay at the dinner table for the entire family meal are much more equipped to behave at Mass than children who are allowed to run around as soon as they're finished eating.

2. Don't Hover. Do Supervise.

Children at this stage should be given the opportunity to try out the socialization skills they learned at home, but they will still need help following through. Resist the temptation to micromanage your child's interactions with other kids. Let them make mistakes. But be close by so that you can intervene when you see emotional temperatures getting to a 7. When you see things going awry, simply bring your child to you and quietly coach them through what to say or do, then send them back to practice while you watch and support.

3. Manage Transitions

About twenty minutes before it's time to leave, tell your kids, "OK guys, we're going to have to leave in about twenty minutes." Tell them again at ten minutes, then give them a five-minute warning. It doesn't matter that they can't tell time or whether you strictly stick to the time limit. The point is, you are giving them time to wrap their heads around leaving. In our experience, most children helped to manage transitions this way get ready to go without a fuss.

4. Debrief and Practice

When you leave a playdate or activity, take some time to talk through how it went after. Start by catching your kids being good. Point out the things your kids handled well. Then, if they did struggle to handle something, this is a good time to problem-solve and practice. Always take the time to role-play new ideas for handling problem situations with peers. Kids need to get these lessons into their muscle memory. Just telling them what to do is a waste of time. They won't remember what you said. Practicing allows them to feel the right thing to do in their bones.

Once your children are in preschool or kindergarten, you can use these same strategies to help them succeed at school.

Getting Ready for School

Most states require children to be enrolled in kindergarten around age five. Whether your children attend school or are homeschooled, the beginning of formal schooling represents an exciting step. Here are a few things to keep in mind to help your children succeed.

You Are – and Will Always Be – the "Primary Educator"

Parents are the "first and foremost educators" of their children.[1] Catholic parents must understand that school exists to support our efforts to educate our children. Don't behave as if school is meant to replace you.

The poet William Butler Yeats famously said, "Education is not the filling of a pail, but the lighting of a fire." Whether your child gets a fire in his belly for learning depends almost entirely on you. In a sense, teaching goes on at school, but learning goes on at home.

In 1966, the US Department of Education studied three thousand schools, six hundred thousand students, and tens of thousands of teachers. The goal was to discover the factors that led to student success. Once factors like income and social class were controlled for, the study showed that no particular type of school or school program exhibited better outcomes than any other. What *did* make a difference? Family. Family structure, family stability, and the degree to which a family was directly involved in children's learning. More recent analyses shows that sixty years on, these findings still hold.[2]

Besides being involved in any homework time (which does happen even at this age), make a point of integrating learning activities into your family life, like reading aloud to your children or taking trips to the museum, the zoo, a working farm, or living history center, etc. Don't just send your kids to activities run by these organizations. Go as a family. Send the message that learning isn't something that happens during school hours, but is the ongoing process of discovering how to celebrate all the wonders God made.

This, again, is why family rituals, especially a weekly "Family Day," are so important. Making time to read, learn, and explore as a family sets kids' hearts ablaze with the joy of discovery.

By all means, pick the nicest, brightest, cleanest, friendliest school for your kids that you can. Just because school environment matters less than family involvement doesn't mean it doesn't matter at all. But keep in mind that the best school for your kids is the one that encourages you to be involved and gives you time to be the close family you want to be. No matter what the school brochure says, the best educational program is the one that goes on in your home.

What About Homeschooling?

For those readers interested in homeschooling, we heartily encourage you to learn more about it. Having been actively involved in homeschooling communities for most of our adult lives, we do want to offer some points to keep in mind.

The first thing is that homeschooling in an attempt to keep your children from the influences of the world is a fool's errand. Most of what we wrote in the section on Rapunzel parenting applies to people who attempt to homeschool for this reason. If it was ever possible (and we doubt that it really was), the internet and digital technology put the last nails in that coffin. The best way to get the benefits homeschooling can offer you and your kids is to approach it as another means of fostering togetherness in your home.

To that end, the most important lesson is that homeschooled kids do best when a parent is actively engaged in teaching the child. Please resist the temptation to place your child in front of a computer while you do … whatever. If your kid's teacher did this in your brick-and-mortar school, you would most likely lead a revolt — and rightly so. The internet can convey information, but children need human interaction to learn and apply it. If you want to homeschool well, one parent is going to have to be a full-time teacher, and you are going to have to divide, hire out, or let go of certain domestic chores just like any other two-career family does. The older your child gets, the truer you will find this to be. Successful homeschooling families recognize that they are, realistically, two-career families.

Finally, it is important to note that homeschooling will magnify your family dynamic at least tenfold. That's not necessarily a bad thing. You just need to expect it and plan to manage the marriage or family problems you may have been ignoring previously. Being intentional about this can help make sure your decision to homeschool benefits every dimension of your family life, not just your children's education.

Teaching How to Pray

Early childhood is a critical stage for laying the foundation for a healthy relationship with God. Faith develops in stages.[3] In order to foster healthy faith development, parents need to understand what spiritual food children need at each age and stage.

Psychologist James Fowler, who identified the Stages of Faith, called this the "Intuitive Projective Stage" of faith development, but you can think of it as the "Cuddly Stage." Basically, kids at this age are wired to believe that something is true and worthwhile if they feel loved, safe, and happy doing it. By contrast, anything they experience as harsh, scary, or punitive will seem worthless and important to resist. Parents who adopt a rigid, formal, overly structured approach to family prayer and faith development may see early compliance from their children who desperately want to please them, but they run the longer-term risk of setting their children up to reject a God (or Church) that feels angry, scary, and out to get them.

At this stage, the most important spiritual lesson a child can learn is that spending time at church and with their family in prayer makes them feel loved, happy, and close to Mom and Dad. This can seem trite to some parents who are serious about their faith, but before children can sit still and learn their prayers and faith facts, they have to encounter a God who loves them, cares about them, makes their family stronger and happier, and can show them how to live a life filled with joy and wonder. Make family prayer time accessible and "cuddly" for your little disciples. Read children's Bible stories together, sing kid-friendly songs about God, cuddle together while you pray, bless your children, and ask God to fill their hearts with his love. Help them see that God's love is *the source* of all the love in your home. For more ideas on how to foster your child's faith through the "Cuddly Stage" (and all the Stages of Faith), check out *Discovering God Together: The Catholic Guide to Raising Faithful Kids.*

Teaching What Love Means

Learning to love as God loves doesn't come naturally. It has to be taught. Early childhood is a great time to start teaching basic lessons about what love really means.

For the Christian, loving someone doesn't mean always feeling warm and fuzzy about them. It means promising to always work for their good and help them be their best. By age five, most children are able to have the following exchange.

> **Child:** I love you, Mommy!
>
> **Mom:** (Gives child a big hug.) Oh, honey, I love you, too. (Big squeeze. Pause.) Hey, let me ask you a question. What does it mean when we say "I love you" to someone?
>
> **Child:** Ummm ... I love you?
>
> **Mom:** Well, sure. Let me ask you this. When I give you big hugs and kisses (big hug and kiss), do I love you then?
>
> **Child:** Yep!
>
> **Mom:** And when we play games and have fun together, does that say, "I love you?"
>
> **Child:** Uh-huh! I like playing puzzles!
>
> **Mom:** I know you do. Me too. But hey, when you get sick and I have to give you that really yucky medicine you don't like, am I loving you?
>
> **Child:** Ummm ... I guess?
>
> **Mom:** You're right. I am loving you then. But what about when you're doing something wrong and I have to correct you? Am I loving you then?
>
> **Child:** Ummm ... yes?
>
> **Mom:** That was a hard one. But you're right. I'm loving you even when I correct you. Gosh, you're smart. Do you know what hugging you, playing with you, giving you medicine when you're sick, and correcting you when you make mistakes all have in

common?

Child: Nuh-uh.

Mom: They're all ways I help you be your best! When we hug and play, I'm helping you feel happy. When I make you take your medicine or even eat vegetables, I'm helping you be healthy and strong. And when I correct you, it's because I want you to be good and get along well with people. Right?

Child: Yeah.

Mom: So, when we say, "I love you" to someone, that means, "I promise to always help you be your best."

This can lead to future discussions about ways your child can help parents, siblings, and others be their best (i.e., love them) by being appropriately affectionate, expressing emotions respectfully, helping with simple chores, playing nicely, and so on.

Early childhood is the stage in which kids start to learn how the world works. A big part of discipling kids involves teaching them how Christians think about love. Teaching them this simple lesson about love and reinforcing it by catching them being good when they behave lovingly is a great way to help your little disciple understand how godly love is different from worldly "love," which is more about using people than helping them be their best. This is why Saint John Paul argued that the opposite of love is not hate, but "use."

For more ideas about helping your children develop healthy attitudes toward love, their bodies, and relationships in early childhood, check out our book *Beyond the Birds and the Bees: Raising Sexually Whole and Holy Kids*.

A Word for Two-Career Families

Everything we describe in this chapter — and really, throughout the book — is even more important for two-career families. Because you have to spend a good chunk of your days apart from one another, and you and your kids are naturally tired and distracted when you get home, it's doubly important that you consciously reconnect every day. The connection between you and your kids won't happen just because it should. It will only happen if you create intentional rituals to facilitate it.

The most important thing to remember as a two-career family is to prioritize your evenings for family connection. Make a point of scheduling a little time to work, play, talk, and pray as a family every single day. As we have discussed previously, this doesn't have to take all night. With a little creativity, you can probably complete all your work, play, talk, and pray ritual time in forty-five to sixty minutes altogether, but you need to make time for it and be intentional about it. This is key to maintaining the connection and rapport that allows you — and not other people — to disciple your kids in your values. Either you can be the one who teaches your kids how a Christian person relates to work, play, relationships, and their spiritual life, or someone/something else will step in.

Plan any extracurricular activities around the time you have left after you schedule time for daily working, playing, talking, and praying rituals. That's important advice for every family, but it is critical for two-career households. *The most important activity is family life.* Nurturing the quality of the relationships in your home is the most effective way to foster healthy socialization in your kids, to disciple them in the habits of a godly lifestyle, and to maintain the rapport that makes good discipline work. Don't be afraid that you are depriving your children by not having them enrolled in three thousand different activities. Give the lion's share of your limited time and energy to being a family first. The rest will follow.

•••

The ages between three and six are a wonderful time for parents and their children. These are the years when you engage in foundational discipleship, laying the groundwork for a healthy emotional life, a godly worldview, and your children's spiritual, relational, and moral imagination.

Prayer

Lord, you said that unless we become like a little child, we cannot enter the kingdom of heaven. Help me see the world through the eyes of my child. Let me be amazed at all your works. Let me join my child in the thrill of discovering the wonders of your world. Help me to respond to my child's questions and concerns as patiently and generously as you respond to mine. Let me innocently depend on you as my child depends on me. Give us the grace to model your love in our home and be witnesses to a godly life.

Holy Family, pray for us. Amen.

Discussion Questions

How is God using this stage of your child's development to help you draw closer to him?

What ideas in this chapter did you find most helpful? Which ideas challenged you?

How will the points in this chapter help you respond to your child with more patience, generosity, and understanding?

CHAPTER 26

Discipling Through Middle Childhood with Grace (Approximately Ages Seven to Ten)

Train the young in the way they should go; even when old, they will not swerve from it.

Proverbs 22:6

What am I good at? What are my gifts? Can I set satisfying goals and meet them despite the obstacles I face? These are the developmental questions that your grade-school-aged disciple needs your help answering.

As you build your House of Discipleship, middle childhood encompasses the years of "vocational discipleship." As John and Claire Grabowski note in *Raising Catholic Kids for Their Vocations*, the word "vocation" comes from the Latin word meaning "to call." We tend to think of a vocation as a call to a specific ministry, like the priesthood, religious life, or marriage and family — and of course, these are vocations. Every "big V" vocation is a call to spend our lives serving others.

231

House of Discipleship

Stage Four: Relational Discipleship (Adolescence)

Teen turns toward parent to develop skills for having godly relationships and finding place in world.

Stage Three: Vocational Discipleship (Middle Childhood)

Child turns toward parent to discover and develop gifts in a way that helps him glorify God and make meaningful contributions to family and others.

Stage Two: Foundational Discipleship (Early Childhood)

Child turns toward parent to learn the stories, rules, and structures that lead to a love-filled, well-ordered life.

Stage One: Embodied Discipleship (Infancy and Toddlerhood)

Child turns toward parent to learn self-regulation and empathy through body-to-body communication.

But before our young disciples can discern their life's vocation, they need our help discovering all the gifts God has given them and learning how to use those gifts to serve others *today.*

Maintaining Attachment Through Middle Childhood

Once kids enter school and start becoming involved in sports, lessons, and other extracurricular activities, it's easy for family life to get squeezed out. As this happens, parents can accidentally give away much of their ability to shape and influence their children's character and worldview. In her controversial book *The Nurture Assumption*, Judith Rich Harris argues that parents matter less than most people think.[1] Her research powerfully showed that, with conventional approaches to parenting, children generally "learn at home how to behave at home ... and they learn outside the home how to behave outside the home."[2] Her argument is that conventional approaches give parents very little influence over their children's behavior, values, and moral attitudes when they walk out the front door of their house. While this may be true for conventional parents, it's not true for parents who adopt a Discipleship Parenting approach. There are three reasons for this.

1. Discipleship Parents are mindful of the need to prioritize family time and safeguard family rituals.

We've repeatedly noted the longstanding research on the power of strong family rituals to help parents maintain influence over their children and pass their faith and values on to their kids. Most conventional parents simply don't have strong family rituals. According to the Bureau of Labor Statistics, most parents of six- to twelve-year-olds spend an average of twenty minutes a day reading, talking, and playing with their children *combined.*[3] On top of this, only 17 percent of Catholic families pray together, and fewer still have even monthly conversations about faith or values.[4] It's difficult to have any influence over our kids if we get no time together and never discuss the things that are supposedly most important to us.

By contrast, even if Discipleship Parents followed our bare minimum recommendation of spending forty-five to sixty minutes a day working, playing, talking, and praying together with their kids, they would be spending two and a half to three times the amount of time with their children as the national average. Even when children are involved in activities, most Discipleship Parenting families will spend much more time together than this because they know how important it is to put family life first. Extracurricular activities are chosen carefully to give kids time to socialize with peers and develop their gifts without jeopardizing the parent-child bond. The increased time Discipleship Parents give to family rituals that model Christian attitudes toward work, leisure, communication, and spirituality give them a much greater ability to form their children than conventional parents have.

2. Discipleship Parents work to maintain strong attachments.

Conventional parents tend not to work on their relationship with their kids until there are problems. Even then, they tend to treat these problems as discipline issues, not as a sign that the relationship needs to be strengthened. As a result, they tend to give away their influence to all the other people (peers, teachers, coaches, media) in their children's lives.

By contrast, Discipleship Parents recognize that their relationship with their kids — like any relationship — requires ongoing care and tending. They also realize that behavior problems are relationship problems first and discipline problems second. Because they are conscious about maintaining both high levels of affection and their commitment to promptly, generously, and consistently respond to their children's needs and concerns, their kids are much more likely to turn to their parents — rather than peers or other adults — with questions about how to handle school, peer, and personal/emotional struggles. They are also much more likely to listen to what their parents say — even over peers and other adults — because they experience their parents actively and intentionally trying to help them meet their needs and lead a healthy, happy life. Secure attachment facilitates a natural "turning toward" impulse that makes kids want to seek out and listen to their parents' advice.

3. Discipleship Parents use proactive, preventive discipline strategies.

Conventional parents tend to use punitive discipline strategies that discourage bad behavior but do not necessarily teach more virtuous alternatives. By contrast, Discipleship Parents assume that their children need to be shepherded and taught proactively. The children of Discipleship Parents experience discipline as helpful instead of shaming. Using their talk ritual time, Discipleship Parents learn about the highs and lows of their kids' days and use discipline strategies like virtue-prompting, rehearsing, role-playing, and others to actively coach their children in handling challenges at school and with peers successfully. This approach to discipline helps Discipleship Parents connect the dots between home and the outside world. It also makes kids more receptive to the lessons their parents are trying to convey. Both of these factors increase Discipleship Parents' influence exponentially.

These three differences in approach and attitude enable Discipleship Parents to actually increase their ability to form their children at the very point most parents are freely giving their influence away. Now let's look at some of the challenges you will be helping your young disciples negotiate in middle childhood.

Middle Childhood: An Overview

There is some overlap with each stage of development as kids continue to master skills learned in an earlier stage and simultaneously turn toward achieving new milestones. To that end, your school-age disciples will continue to develop their capacity for emotional integration and purposeful action. Additionally, they'll direct more energy toward identifying their gifts, learning to use those gifts in godly, pro-social ways, and fostering consistent follow-through.

At Age Seven

At seven, children reach the "age of reason." They're now consistently able to connect actions and consequences and understand the basic reasons behind the rules. As far as the Church is concerned, this is also the first time children are capable of actually committing a sin. Prior to this, children's misbehavior could not be considered sinful. In order to sin you need to be fully aware of the negative impact of your actions and intentionally choose that path anyway. Children younger than seven cannot do this consistently.

Cognitively, your child is beginning to think in more complex, though still concrete, ways. For instance, your child used to think that cutting up their food into smaller pieces meant that you were giving them more food. Now they understand that there are simply more bites of the same amount of food.

Likewise, children at this age are less literal. They have a better sense of what you are saying to them. For instance, if you told your five-year-old to stop tapping on the table, he might say, "I'm NOT tapping on the table," because, in his mind, he is playing the drums. The five-year-old isn't lying. He honestly doesn't understand why you don't know that he is pretending to be the drummer in his favorite band. The seven-year-old, however, can understand that "tapping on the table" covers a multitude of annoying behaviors.

If they haven't shown this yet, some kids can get a little scrupulous at this age. Because they can now connect the dots to see how many things they do are potentially annoying or upsetting, they may worry that they are being upsetting or annoying — or even sinful — all the time. The best way to deal with this is to not argue with the child. Instead, decrease their baseline emotional temperature by ramping up your affection, and be sure to increase the frequency with which you catch them being good. When these episodes of scrupulosity come, hold them in your arms and give them time-in. Remind them how much you love them even when they feel bad inside. Pray with them and remind them how much God loves them. Help them identify the little things that go right in the day that are examples of "God's hugs." Surround them with your love and God's to bring them back online. For most kids, this will be enough. If the scrupulosity persists for several weeks after trying this approach, it may be time to get a professional evaluation.

At Age Eight

Many eight-year-olds combine an increasingly outgoing nature with a surprisingly more intense relationship with Mom (in particular). Think of this as a mini-revisiting of toddlerhood. As the child ventures even further out, he needs more reassurance that his home base is secure. Be patient with this. Ramp up the affection. Strengthen family rituals. Offer ample encouragement. Be careful not to shame the child for his or her tentativeness while gently and consistently encouraging appropriate risks, such as trying new activities or meeting new kids. Children who are more shy by nature can become more social if you first help them become confident in one-on-one playdates, and then smaller groups of two or three before making them deal with larger groups. The stronger your bond with the child and the more able you are to set up situations where success can build on success, the more your children will take their independence when they are ready.

Age Nine Plus

At ages nine and ten, your child is becoming more self-motivated and goal-directed. This is also the stage where you can begin expecting your child to follow through on tasks without you having to check up on every part of the process. They will still need some support and direction, and they will still need you to follow through, but you should be able to trust them not to forget your instructions by the time they walk from one room to the other.

Continuing to Develop Emotional Maturity

In early childhood, you were primarily focused on getting your child to take the first steps toward more independent emotional control and coming alongside of you to learn how to do various household tasks. In middle childhood your main tasks are helping your child fine-tune their ability to express emotions in healthy ways and building on their growing capacity for follow-through.

Fostering Emotional Maturity

If you have been using the emotional redirection/emotional temperature techniques we have been teaching throughout this book, your child should be well on their way to expressing feelings respectfully. Even then, every child has bad moments, and some children more than others. Seven-year-olds may still tantrum, but these tantrums are usually less the result of being emotionally overwhelmed and more about manipulation.

Here is a simple way to test whether your seven-year-old's tantrums are the result of delayed emotional maturity (in which case they continue to need the support you gave throughout early childhood), or whether they are more manipulative in nature. Does your child stop his outburst/

tantrum and resort to being pleasant almost immediately after being granted their request?

If the answer is "no," then your child is truly overwrought and needs ongoing support. Their feelings are probably very strong, and it is just going to take them a little longer than other kids to learn to manage them consistently and well.

If the answer is "yes," then you are being manipulated. When your child makes a request, be thoughtful and give your answer. If your child becomes upset, simply say something like, "I understand that you are upset, but I've given you my answer. You may either calm down and stop fussing or you can take a time-out to cool yourself down (or lose the privilege associated with the tantrum as a logical consequence). Which do you prefer?"

These suggestions should help most children develop the ability to express their emotions in healthy ways. If your child's tantrums either happen so often or become so elevated that you are doubting your ability to help them, professional help may be indicated.

Developing "Industry" (Follow-Through)

Being able to set goals and meet them despite the obstacles that we may encounter is a key task of middle childhood. The ability to demonstrate fortitude (a.k.a., "industry" or "self-efficacy") — that is, good follow-through in the face of adversity — is the most important component of self-esteem. If your kids are confident in their ability to set and achieve their goals despite the obstacles life throws in their path, they'll feel competent and confident. If they question their ability to set and achieve their goals consistently, they will feel incompetent, confused, and resistant to new opportunities to challenge themselves. Here are some ways you can disciple your kids through the process of fostering fortitude.

Give Children More Independent Responsibilities

In toddlerhood, children played at doing chores. Their efforts were more focused on being near their mommy and daddy and playing "being helpful." That's the first step to actually learning how to be helpful.

In early childhood, they began working at your side, learning how to actually do chores to your standards and discovering that doing chores was one way to build relationship with you and show their love for you.

Now, in middle childhood, kids understand your expectations enough to begin to be asked to do some chores themselves. If you haven't worked side-by-side with them on a particular chore before, start there. For instance, instead of just expecting that they should be able to clean their rooms perfectly just because you told them to do it, clean their room together a few times. Praise them for their hard work. Each time you work together, give them more responsibility for handling the various tasks associated with the chore before asking them to take it on themselves. Let success build on success. This is the process of discipleship.

Once your young disciple has mastered a task working beside you, assign some of these responsibilities to be their personal chores. Don't give up family work rituals altogether. Rather, identify a separate list of ways your child can personally contribute to the good of your household in addition to the work rituals you have as a family. Be sure to praise them for jobs well done and gently encourage them to stick with it when their efforts are lagging. Don't ever let chores turn into a power struggle. Deal with tantrums as we described above and in the discipline section. Empathize but be firm. Help them over the emotional hump and require them to finish their job when they are calm. Don't ever do their jobs for them.

Cultivate greater responsibility and generosity in your young disciple by teaching them that chores aren't done *until they come back to you and ask you to check their work.* Show you care by checking to make sure their efforts are up to your standards. Reward a job well done with genuine praise and affection. Enforce the need to have you to check their work with logical consequences. For instance, if you told your child that they can't go to practice until the chore is done, and they haven't asked you to check it, don't take them to practice. Make them ask you to review what they have done. Have them take care of anything they may have missed. Then take them. If they're late, they're late. If they miss practice (or the game, etc.), they miss it. The "home team" comes first. Always.

You don't have to yell. The logical consequences of a few late arrivals to events are all most kids will need to remember that they need to seek your approval before moving on to something else. Another good habit to teach your child is that, at the end of everything they do, they should ask, "Is there anything else I can do for you?" Your children can do this if you teach them. This is the level of service and virtuous self-giving that is possible with Discipleship Parenting. Expecting children to serve the family as generously as you serve them is what prevents spoiling.

These habits teach your children that an attitude of generosity is even more important than just getting the chore done. Don't let your family just *say* you love one another. Back up that promise to work for one another's good by actually insisting that you work for one another's good.

Help Kids Manage Their Emotional Temps in the Face of New Challenges

An important part of discipling your kids in middle childhood is teaching them appropriate ways to challenge themselves. Gifts don't grow if they are left untried. It is important to encourage children to try new lessons, activities, and social opportunities even when they are reluctant to do so.

Related to this, many parents wonder how hard they can "push" their kids, for instance, to complete homework, try new activities, develop new friendships, or challenge themselves in new ways. Also, since middle childhood is the critical stage for learning follow-through, is it ever OK to just let them quit something that's not working out?

A good rule of thumb is that you can push your kids (or ask them to stick with something) to the degree that you can help them keep their emotional temperature at a 7 or lower. That doesn't mean that if your child's emotional temperature ever rises above that point you should let them off the hook for doing something. It just means that any guidance you offer will only be received at a 7 or below. Likewise, an activity is only beneficial if the child can keep their emotional temperature at a 7 or lower while they are doing it. Any higher and the child isn't learning anything from the experience. At a 7+, your child's thinking brain is flooding. By 8 their emotional brain is on overload, and they are merely surviving the experience, counting the seconds until it is over. They learn nothing and receive no benefit from it.

To help your child keep their emotional temperature low in the face of a challenge, use ample affection and encouragement; remind your child of past successes; help your child pray — preferably, in their own words — for God to help them find both the gifts they need to apply to the situation and the strength to continue; and ask leading questions that point to solutions without spoon-feeding them answers.

On the other hand, some activities just aren't meant for some kids. For instance, a client of ours wanted her child to take piano lessons, but something about playing the piano just caused the eight-year-old to emotionally flood almost immediately. Her parents tried every trick in the book, but they couldn't get her to do anything but power through lessons and battle through practice. She was learning nothing, and the experience of trying to help her manage her moods around the lessons practically wrecked the entire day. In a situation like this, the best thing to do is to say something like, "Music is important to us and we need you to do something musical, but we won't make you stick with piano if you can give us an instrument you would like to learn."

Under this approach, their daughter eventually chose voice lessons. These lessons went well and helped the young lady get the benefits of a musical education without the hellish torture of piano lessons. Succeeding with voice, she recently asked to take guitar, too.

Learning follow-through doesn't always mean having to stick with this exact thing no matter what. It means learning to stick with something to the degree that it is possible to do it while keeping your emotional temperature in check. Or, when that isn't possible, choosing a similar activity and learning to stick with that. In this way children can be taught to value the activities that are important to their parents while still having the freedom to explore their own interests.

Developing Good Study Habits

Another important part of discipling your child in the virtue of fortitude is helping them develop good study habits. God wants his children to use their minds to discover the world he has created for them and to find their place in it. Children don't need straight A's to accomplish this, but they have to be disciplined, tenacious learners with good study habits. These are not skills that every child is born with, but they are skills that, with patience and gentle guidance from Mom and Dad, every child can learn. Here are some best practices to foster good follow-through with school work.

Be Aware and Involved in School Life

Take an active interest in your child's school life and what they're learning. Volunteer as you are able. Become familiar with the online learning platform your child's school uses. Get to know your child's teachers. Give them a way to contact you with any questions or concerns. Don't wait until parent-teacher conferences to ask how your child is doing. Don't hound your kid's teachers or undermine their authority, but do be appropriately engaged. Let your child know — through your investment of time and energy — that their education is important to you.

You, Not the School, Are in Charge of Homework

Don't ever passively accept your children's claims that they know a subject well, that they have completed their homework successfully, or that they "don't have any homework." Be the "head teacher." Make it clear from the earliest school age that your kids are not working to meet their teacher's standards, but yours. Children learn best with consistent expectations, but teachers change from year to year. You are the constant in your child's life. Give your children the gift of consistent expectations for their classroom behavior and academic performance. Often, your standards will be higher than their teachers', sometimes not. Either way, let your child know that your standards are the ones that matter. When you check their homework, don't hesitate to gently and charitably insist that they redo anything that is not up to your standard. Actively support your child in using the brain God gave them to the best of their ability. Use their emotional temperature as your guide for how much to press. Be gentle. Be supportive. Be calm. But set the standard.

Establish Daily Homework Time

A good work ritual to have is daily homework time — not just for the kids, but for you too! Schedule at least thirty to forty-five minutes per evening sitting around the kitchen table together while your kids do homework and you pay bills, do paperwork, catch up on emails, fold laundry, or even just read. This way, you're available to provide support and supervision even while you're modeling good work habits. It's hard for kids to concentrate on their work when the rest of the family is relaxing or playing. Make a point of being a team that supports one another in getting your respective work done.

Requiring at least thirty minutes of study time per night eliminates the struggle with kids "forgetting" homework. Let your children know that you expect them to bring home something to study every evening — even when they don't have "official homework" — or you will assign them something to study or read. Let them know you will review it with them after as well, just like you do their homework. Don't present this as a punishment. Simply state it as a necessity for developing good learning habits. A study of 43,000 grade-school students found that children who read every day performed significantly better on every measure of academic achievement.[5] Give your kids the advantage of regular learning time at home.

When you do assign work, make sure it is relevant to what they are studying in school. Become familiar with their books. Make a point of acquiring supplemental learning materials that help them go a little deeper into whatever they are learning at school. Once kids realize that you will require them to study for at least thirty minutes per night regardless of whether the teacher has assigned anything, they'll be sure to stop "forgetting" to bring home the work they're going to get classroom credit for. Plus, they might just surprise themselves and enjoy learning new things and getting better grades for the extra effort. Discipleship Parents should be concerned about learning, not just "getting stuff done." Daily family study/homework time creates a household where learning, responsibility, conscientiousness, and stewardship are modeled, prized, and practiced.

•••

Whether you call it industry, follow-through, or the good old-fashioned virtue of fortitude, the practices we've been describing help you disciple your child through the process of setting goals and meeting them even in the face of frustrations and challenges. Believe it or not, every one of these lessons has ramifications for your kids' spiritual life. It's tough to be faithful in today's world. Every opportunity to grow in fortitude will directly impact your child's ability to live a meaningful, dynamic faith life despite adversity. Let's explore ways to foster your child's spirituality through middle childhood.

Fostering Your Child's Spiritual Life

Middle childhood encompasses the "Story and Structure Stage" of faith development (aka, the "Mythic-Literal Stage"). In early childhood, children primarily consider story time a source of entertainment and connection with Mom and Dad. In middle childhood, children begin to learn and apply life lessons from the stories you read. In our digital and media-driven age, stories are all around us 24/7 in the form of TV programs, movies, internet videos, and the like. The best chance a Christian parent has for competing with these more worldly stories and lessons is creating a regular, daily reading ritual — either at bedtime or some other time. This is not just for small children and picture books. Even when kids can read on their own, parents should be reading age-appropriate chapter books together with their children each night. A daily reading time allows you to read your kids stories that either convey your faith and values, affirm your faith and values, or give you nonthreatening ways to discuss challenges to your faith and values as you explore the choices the characters make in the stories you read together.

The Spiritual Benefits of Rituals

Structures continue to be important in middle childhood. Grade-school children need a scaffolding to help them build a balanced and well-rounded life. This stage is really your last chance to establish family rituals without encountering significant pushback from your kids. Without strong family work, play, talk, and pray rituals, children simply reach out to TV, the internet, and bad habits to fill their time. By contrast, the stronger your rituals for working, playing, talking, and praying are in your family, the more you'll be able to effectively model healthy Christian attitudes toward work, leisure, relationships, and faith.

Virtue-Based Discipline

It's important at this stage to start asking virtue-based questions when disciplining your kids. Instead of telling your child what to do, ask them,

"What do you think the most loving/responsible/generous/kind/etc. thing to do would be?" Build your young disciples' capacity for moral reasoning by making them think through their choices and praising them for the effort they put into discerning the right thing to do. The closer your children get to being preteens and adolescents, the more important it will be to adopt this more Socratic, virtue-based approach to discipline as opposed to simply telling your kids what to do.

Foster A Richer Moral and Spiritual Life

Even though the grade-school child's faith is more thoughtful (as opposed to emotional), it is still fairly simplistic. As they move through middle childhood toward the preteen years, children move from black-and-white moral reasoning to more sophisticated questions. To facilitate this maturation, make a point of reading and discussing Bible stories that seem to contradict each other (for instance, the parable of the prodigal son and the parable of the unmerciful servant). Or read stories that present age-appropriate moral dilemmas. Help your kids develop their capacity to think in more sophisticated ways about applying faith and moral lessons to real-life challenges.

At this stage, children also need to encounter a God who doesn't mind getting his hands dirty; a God who walks with them all day long and is present in all their struggles and all their joys. In addition to the formal prayers you may say as a family (grace at meals, the Rosary, etc.), help your children learn to talk to God as the person who knows them best and loves them most. Lead them through the process of thanking him for the little blessings throughout the day and asking him for help when they're having a tough time with school or peers. Sometimes, ask them to lead in their own words. When they come to you with questions or concerns, after you comfort them yourself, help them pray that God would let them figure out the best way to respond, then discuss possible answers together. As long as the problems exist, keep praying this way. When the problems eventually get resolved, help your kids thank God for his guidance and praise him for helping them through tough times.

Don't Outsource Your Kids' Faith Development

It has been our observation that Catholic parents tend to assume that youth groups or teen conferences are the places kids will "catch" a love for their faith. Unconsciously, many faithful parents assume that they are competent enough to build the machine of faith — (i.e., faith facts and religious habits) — but then they must hire a licensed spiritual electrician (a youth minister or conference speaker) to plug in the machine. This is a tragic mistake. Too many children are lost because they never meet the person outside their family who can give them a real encounter with Christ.

It is *your primary job* as a Catholic parent to give your child a personal relationship with Jesus Christ, a deep experience of God's love, and a deep understanding that God wants to be involved in their everyday lives. We certainly pray that, as your children grow and mature, they will meet other faithful young people, become involved in dynamic youth groups, and encounter other faithful adults who can show them how to deepen the spiritual life you have fostered in your kids. But don't think for one minute that it is anyone's responsibility but yours to light the fire of faith in your child's heart. If you don't do it, you're effectively leaving it to chance.

The preteen and teen years are the time when kids carry the spiritual fire that Mom and Dad have already kindled in their hearts out to the world at large. Without that fire, lit from your family's spiritual hearth, the preteen and teen years can be a very cold, scary time. Middle childhood is the time to introduce your children to a personal, loving, incarnate God. A God who longs to be involved in every part of their life and wants to celebrate their good times, comfort them in the bad times, and counsel them through the confusing times. The tips in this section will get you started, but we discuss more tips for fostering your grade-school child's spiritual life in *Discovering God Together: The Catholic Guide to Raising Faithful Kids.*

Fostering Healthy Sexual Identity

Another major task in middle childhood is helping your children to develop a healthy sexual identity. In particular, your young disciple needs help understanding what it means to be a boy or a girl who feels confident and secure in his or her own skin.

Secular society offers many competing ideas about what it means to be a boy or a girl. In this marketplace of ideas, Saint John Paul II's Theology of the Body is a critical resource for parents who want to cultivate a healthy, non-repressive, Christian view of sexual identity.

Many people have the attitude that one's sexuality is determined by the interests one has, the things one does, the feelings one has, or the activities a person is drawn to. Many Christians buy into this mindset as well. The affectionate, empathetic boy who likes to sing instead of play sports is told he is effeminate and made to feel he isn't man enough. The self-disciplined girl who likes to build things instead of playing dress-up is made to feel there is something wrong with her. A great deal of gender confusion is caused by parents who try to force their children into too narrow, "traditional" stereotypes of what constitutes a healthy male or female identity. In fact, these categories have very little to do with the Christian view of the person.

The Theology of the Body teaches that masculinity or femininity are not dependent on what you like, what you do, or even how you feel. It is dependent upon how you are made. You ARE a man because you have a male body. You ARE a woman because you have a female body. You don't have to "become" a man or woman (as we so often, unfortunately, tell our children they have to do). God made it so. A man IS masculine when he uses his male body to love and serve others. A woman IS feminine when she uses her female body to love and serve others. Masculinity and femininity are gifts from God that we develop through loving service to others. We do not become manly or womanly by cramming ourselves into culturally defined categories regarding likes, feelings, preferences, and habits. We do not lose our masculinity or femininity because we do not fit into those culturally defined categories. Our sexuality is a gift from God, not the culture. Men are manly when they use the gifts, talents, and body God has given them to work for the good of others, to care for them, and to build them up. Women are womanly when they do the same with the gifts, talents, and bodies God gave them. The more we develop all the virtues that make us fully formed human persons, and express those virtues through the body God has given us, the more we cultivate authentic masculinity or femininity.

Help your children praise God for the body he has given them and all the wonderful things they can do with their body and mind. Likewise, teach them to generously love and serve others and work for their good. In response to this loving, embodied service, their own secure sense of masculinity or femininity will emerge as a gift from God entirely separate from whether they like ballet or sports, need more hugs or roughhousing time, like to play dress-up or build things, or ... whatever.

There is much more that can and should be said about this topic than space permits in this book. We discuss many more ways to foster healthy sexual identity in middle childhood in our book, *Beyond the Birds and the Bees: Raising Sexually Whole and Holy Kids.*

• • •

Discipling your child through middle childhood involves helping your child understand how a Christian person is meant to think about the gifts that God has given him, how he uses those gifts to bless those around him, and how to rely on those gifts to achieve goals in the face of adversity. In middle childhood, Discipleship Parents also lay the groundwork for healthy moral reasoning, a personally meaningful connection with God and faith, and the beginnings of a secure sexual identity.

In your House of Discipleship, middle childhood is your opportunity to give your child a rightly ordered sense of self and a healthy relationship with God. Let middle childhood be the time when you kindle the fire of faith in your child's heart so that he or she can enter the preteen and teen years discovering how to set the world ablaze with God's love.

Prayer
Lord, as I help my children discover their talents and how to use them to both glorify you and work for the good of others, help me to see all the ways you are working in, through, and with me to bless my family. Help me to appreciate how wonderfully I am made and to look for more ways to use everything you have given me to serve those you have placed in my care. As I serve my family, make me mindful of all the ways you take care of me and how you always make time to love, help, and support me when I am most in need.

Holy Family, pray for us. Amen.

Discussion Questions

How is God using your relationship with your grade-school child to help you draw closer to him?

Which ideas did you find most useful in this chapter? Which ideas challenged you?

How will you use the things you learned in this chapter to strengthen your relationship with your grade-school-aged child?

CONCLUSION

Living the Liturgy of Domestic Church Life

In the Eucharist the sacrifice of Christ becomes also
the sacrifice of the members of his Body. The lives
of the faithful, their praise, sufferings, prayer, and
work, are united with those of Christ and with his
total offering, and so acquire a new value.

CCC 1368

Thank you for allowing us to accompany you on this part of your parenting journey. We hope you'll let us walk with you through the preteen and teen years in *Parenting Your Teens and Tweens with Grace.* For now, we hope you can see what a radically different, radically faithful system Discipleship Parenting is.

The most important takeaway from this book is that, for Catholics especially, parenting isn't just about parenting. It is, ultimately, a spiritual exercise; a participation in the celebration of what could be called the Liturgy of Domestic Church Life. We first introduced this idea back in chapter three. We'd like to offer some final suggestions for celebrating this liturgy in full and unlocking the spiritual potential of your family.

Celebrating the Liturgy of Domestic Church Life

Recall we said that liturgy is the work God does through the Church to heal the damage that sin does to our relationships with him and others. In the Liturgy of the Eucharist, God restores our union with him and makes communion with others possible. By extension, the Liturgy of Domestic Church Life allows us to bring Jesus home and make our faith the source of the warmth in our home. Through the Liturgy of Domestic Church Life, our broken, sinful, struggling families are consecrated to Christ and equipped to become something sacred and divine — dynamic domestic churches! The Holy Spirit enables you to fill your home with Christ's love, allows every aspect of family life to be filled with God's grace, and ultimately empowers you to consecrate the world to Christ. (If you're interested in understanding the theological basis for this Liturgy of Domestic Church Life, please see *Renewing Catholic Family Life*, the book produced by the Symposium on Catholic Family Life and Spirituality.)

Getting Family Life "Rite"

All the "stuff" Discipleship Parents do all day is not just spiritual, it's liturgical. That is to say, it's meant to help parents do our part to cooperate with God's grace and heal the damage sin has done to our human relationships — especially in our homes. Everything we do all day is ministry, if we do it with the intention of communicating God's love to our spouse and kids.

That said, a liturgy is composed of various rites, which are, in a sense, the building blocks of liturgy. For instance, the Liturgy of the Eucharist has an opening rite, a penitential rite, an offertory rite, a Communion rite, and a concluding rite, just to name a few. These rites guide us through a meaningful celebration of the Eucharist. The absence of any of these rites could negatively impact the quality, integrity, or even validity of the Mass.

Although we haven't categorized them in this way before now, most of this book has actually been describing the three rites of the Liturgy of Domestic Church Life. They are the Rite of Christian Relationship, the Rite of Family Rituals, and the Rite of Reaching Out. Each of these rites helps parents and kids live out different aspects of their baptismal mission to be priests, prophets, and royals:

- *The Rite of Christian Relationship:* A priest's job is to offer sacrifices that make things holy and build a bridge between heaven and earth. Godly families live out the priestly mission of their baptism by loving one another, not just with the love that comes naturally to us as broken, sinful people, but with sacrificial, Christian love. When Christian families intentionally make little sacrifices to work for one another's good throughout the day, we consecrate our homes to Christ, help one another become holy, and make our homes a sacred space. Our common, messy, crazy households become domestic churches.
- *The Rite of Family Rituals:* A prophet is someone who reminds God's people how they are meant to live. When we make a little time to work, play, talk, and pray together every day, we model how Christians are meant to relate to work, leisure, relationships, and faith and witness to the world how Christians are called to live. This is the main way parents and kids can help one another practice the prophetic mission of our baptism.
- *The Rite of Reaching Out:* To serve with Christ is to reign with him. As Christians, we're meant to be a blessing to others. When we go about our day keeping others in mind, being kind, charitable, hospitable, serving others, and discerning our family mission and charisms, we serve with Christ and build the kingdom of God. Practicing the Rite of Reaching Out is the main way parents and kids help one another practice the royal mission of our baptism.

Each of these rites contributes something important to your domestic church's ability to be happy, healthy, and to experience every part (even the messy parts) of family life as sacred. By understanding how the various practices we've described in this book fit into the three rites of the Liturgy of Domestic Church Life, you can see how every part of your parenting life is meant to be a prayer.

Liturgy of Domestic Church Life Quiz

The following quiz can help summarize the different practices associated with the Liturgy of Domestic Church Life and give you a way to assess your family's strengths and areas for growth. Rate your family on a scale of 1 ("We don't do this at all") to 5 ("This describes us perfectly!").

How Does Our Family Live the Rite of Christian Relationship?

Through the Rite of Christian Relationship, Catholic families live the *priestly mission of their baptism* by practicing the sacrificial love that comes from God's heart. Although every family is different, there are some things every family can do to live this rite in full:

___a. We prioritize family time. Because we can only form godly kids if we spend meaningful time together every day, we don't let outside activities compete with our efforts to create a close-knit, family team.

___b. We are extravagantly affectionate. Christ's love is generous and incarnate. As a Christian household, we imitate Christ by being generously and appropriately affectionate, affirming, and supportive of one another.

___c. Pope Saint John Paul II said that Christian relationships are characterized by "mutual self-giving." We work hard to respond to one another's needs (parents and kids), promptly, generously, consistently, and cheerfully.

___d. We practice discipleship discipline in our home. As Saint John Bosco taught, we reject harsh punishments and focus on teaching, supporting, and encouraging godly behavior through "reason, religion, and loving-kindness."

Just imagine how millions of families practicing the above habits could change the world by conveying a truly beautiful, intimate vision of family life. That is the priestly fruit of the Liturgy of Domestic Church Life.

How Does Our Family Live the Rite of Family Rituals?

Through the Rite of Family Rituals, Catholic families live the *prophetic mission of baptism* by developing strong family rituals that model Christian attitudes toward work, leisure, relationships, and prayer. Although every family is different, there are some things every family can do to live this rite in full:

___a. Work rituals. Each day, instead of dividing and conquering, we make time to do at least some household chores together. We don't think of chores as just "things that have to get done." We know they are opportunities to learn to be a team and take good care of one another.

___b. Play rituals. Every day, we make a point to play together, enjoy one another's company, and model healthy ways to celebrate our life together.

___c. Talk rituals. Several times a week, we have meaningful conversations (not lectures) about faith, values, how God is showing up for us, and how we can take better care of one another.

___d. Prayer rituals. We pray together as a family throughout each day. We relate to Jesus as another member of our family. We regularly praise him and ask for his help.

Imagine the difference millions of families who dedicated themselves to modeling an authentic Christian approach to work, play, relationships, and God would make. That is the prophetic fruit of the Liturgy of Domestic Church Life.

How Does Our Family Live the Rite of Reaching Out?

Through the Rite of Reaching Out, Catholic families live the *royal mission of their baptism* by cultivating a spirit of loving service inside and outside the home. Although it's important to find ways to serve your parish or community together as a family, true Christian service begins at home and extends outward. Every family is different, but there are some things every family can do to live this rite in full:

___a. We take good care of one another at home. Authentic Christian service begins with caring generously for the people under our roof.

___b. We think about others even when we're home. As a family, we donate our gently used items, look for ways to help our neighbors, and make our home a place where others can enjoy godly fun and fellowship.

___c. We are kind, thoughtful, and use good manners in and outside our home. As a family, we're conscious of leaving people happier than we found them.

___d. We regularly engage in charitable service together as a family.

Imagine the impact of millions of Catholic families intentionally looking for ways to cheerfully serve one another and work together to make a positive difference in their parishes and communities. That is the royal fruit of the Liturgy of Domestic Church Life.

How'd You Do?

Every family has its own strengths and areas for growth. Use this quiz to guide discussions in your family about what you're doing well and what you'd like to work on next. The more you live out the Liturgy of Domestic Church Life, the easier it will be for your family to get a clear picture of both your family mission and charism as well.

In on the Secret

So now you're in on our not-so-little secret. *Parenting Your Kids with Grace* isn't really a parenting book at all. At least not the way most people think about parenting books. It is meant to be a guide to encountering God's love more fully in your home and changing the world through the ministry of parenting.

As you apply our suggestions and discern the best way to celebrate the Liturgy of Domestic Church Life in your family, we pray that God will abundantly bless you and your children. May the Lord lead you — day by day — to a deeper experience of his love flowing through your home. And may the Lord lead you to a greater awareness of the amazing ways he wants to use your family to be a blessing to others through the witness of your lives.

Yours in Christ,
Dr. Greg & Lisa Popcak,
Jacob Popcak, MA, & Rachael Isaac, MSW

Need a Hand? Let Us Help!

Dear Reader,

It can be challenging to be a faithful parent, but you don't have to go it alone. If you find yourself struggling with personal, emotional, spiritual, or relational problems that make it difficult to be the joyful, peaceful, grace-filled person or parent you long to be, we are here to help you on your journey.

Since 1999, the Pastoral Solutions Institute (www.CatholicCounselors.com) has offered Catholic-integrated tele-counseling services for Catholic individuals, couples, and families around the world. All of our therapists are fully licensed, have additional training in pastoral theology, and are completely faithful to the teachings of the Church.

We combine the best techniques counseling psychology has to offer with the timeless wisdom of our Catholic faith to help you heal your wounds and achieve your goals. To learn more about how we can help you, visit us online at CatholicCounselors.com. We look forward to helping you take the next step on your journey toward a more abundant marriage, family, or personal life.

Sincerely,
Dr. Greg Popcak
Executive Director
Pastoral Solutions Institute
www.CatholicCounselors.com

References

Ainsworth, Mary, Mary Blehar, Everett Waters, and Sally N. Wall. *Patterns of Attachment: A Psychological Study of the Strange Situation.* New York: Routledge, 2015.

American Academy of Pediatrics. "Parent-child Reading and Story Time Promote Brain Development prior to Kindergarten," 2014.

American Academy of Pediatrics. "American Academy of Pediatrics Announces Safe Sleep Recommendations to Protect Against SIDS," 2016.

American Academy of Pediatrics. "Breastfeeding and the Use of Human Milk." *Pediatrics* 129, no. 3, March 2012.

Barger, Jan. "Is It Strange to Still Be Nursing My 2-year-old?" Babycenter .com. https://www.babycenter.com/toddler/feeding/is-it-strange-to -still-be-nursing-my-2-year-old_4759#.

Bartkus, Justin, and Christian Smith. "A Report on American Catholic Religious Parenting." Notre Dame, IN: McGrath Institute for Church Life, 2015.

Beck, C. T. "Predictors of Postpartum Depression: An Update." *Nursing Research* 50, no. 5 (September–October 2001): 275–85.

Belfort, Mandy Brown. "The Science of Breastfeeding and Brain Development." *Breastfeeding Medicine* 12, no. 8 (August 2017).

Bengtson, Vern L. *Families and Faith: How Religion Is Passed Down across Generations.* Oxford: Oxford University Press, 2017.

Bowlby, John. *A Secure Base: Parent-Child Attachment and Healthy Human Development.* New York: Basic Books, 1999.

Cameron-Smith, Kim. *Discipleship Parenting: Planting the Seeds of*

Faith. Huntington, IN: OSV, 2019.

"Workaholic Fathers Are Turning Children into 'Orphans,' Says Francis." *Catholic Herald,* January 28, 2015.

Clinton, Tim, and Joshua Straub. *God Attachment: Why You Believe, Act, and Feel the Way You Do about God.* Brentwood, TN: Howard Books, 2014.

Clinton, Tim, and Gary Sibcy. *Attachments: Why You Love, Feel, and Act the Way You Do.* Nashville: Thomas Nelson, 2009.

Cozolino, Louis. *The Neuroscience of Human Relationships: Attachment and the Developing Social Brain.* New York: W. W. Norton & Co., 2014.

Dwyer, Carol, Carol Dweck, and Heather Carlson-Jaquez. "Using Praise to Enhance Student Resilience and Learning Outcomes." American Psychological Association, 2010. https://www.apa.org/education /k12/using-praise.

Egalite, Anna. "How Family Background Influences Student Achievement." *Education Next* 16, no. 2 (February 17, 2016).

Fiese, Barbara H. *Family Routines and Rituals.* New Haven, CT: Yale University Press, 2006.

Grabowski, John and Claire. *Raising Catholic Kids for Their Vocations.* Charlotte, NC: Tan, 2019.

Gray, Mark. "The Catholic Family: 21st Century Challenges in the United States." CARA and Holy Cross Family Ministries, June 2015. https://cara.georgetown.edu/staff/webpages/CatholicFamilyResearch.pdf.

Harris, Judith Rich. *The Nurture Assumption: Why Children Turn Out the Way They Do.* Revised and updated. New York: Free Press, 2009.

Hart, Jonathan, Alicia Limke, and Phillip R. Budd. "Attachment and Faith Development." *Journal of Psychology and Theology* 36, no. 2 (2010).

Jerrim, John, Luis Alejandro Lopez-Agudo, and Oscar D. Marcenaro-Gutierrez. "Does It Matter What Children Read? New Evidence Using Longitudinal Census Data from Spain." *Oxford Review of Education* 46, no. 5 (February 27, 2020).

Krol, Kathleen M., and Tobias Grossmann. "Psychological Effects of

Breastfeeding on Children and Mothers." *Bundesgesundheitsblatt Gesundheitsforschung Gesundheitsschutz*, June 22, 2018.

Lehrer, Jonah. "Do Parents Matter?" *Scientific American*, April 9, 2009. https://www.scientificamerican.com/article/parents-peers -children/#.

Maselko, J., L. Kubzansky, L. Lipsitt, and S. L. Buka. "Mother's Affection at 8 Months Predicts Emotional Distress in Adulthood." *Journal of Epidemiology and Community Health* 65, no. 7 (2011).

Maslach, Christina, and Michael P. Leiter. "Understanding the Burnout Experience: Recent Research and Its Implications for Psychiatry." *World Psychiatry* 15, no. 2 (June 2016): 103–11.

Mayo Clinic Staff. "Chronic Stress Puts Your Health at Risk." Healthy Lifestyle: Stress Management, March 19, 2019. https://www .mayoclinic.org/healthy-lifestyle/stress-management/in-depth /stress/art-20046037.

McCarthy, Claire, M.D. "New Study Says that It's OK to Let Babies Cry at Night." *Harvard Health Blog*, May 31, 2016. https://www.health .harvard.edu/blog/new-study-says-okay-let-babies-cry -night-201605319774#.

McKenna, James J., Ph.D. Mother-Baby Behavioral Sleep Laboratory. University of Notre Dame, https://cosleeping.nd.edu.

Mendelsohn, Alan, Carolyn Brockmeyer Cates, Adriana Weisleder, Samantha Berkule Johnson, Anne M. Seery, Caitlin F. Canfield, Harris S. Huberman, and Bernard P. Dreyer. "Reading Aloud, Play, and Social-Emotional Development." *Pediatrics* 141, no. 5 (May 2018).

Middlemiss, Wendy, Douglas A. Granger, Wendy A. Goldberg, and Laura Nathans. "Asynchrony of Mother-Infant Hypothalamic-Pituitary-Adrenal Axis Activity Following Extinction of Infant Crying Responses Induced During the Transition to Sleep." *Early Human Development* 88, no. 4 (April 2012): 227–32.

Muza, Sharon. "Exclusively Breastfeeding Mothers Get More Sleep: Another Look at Nighttime Breastfeeding and Postpartum Depression." *Connecting the Dots: Research and Resources for Perinatal Professionals*. Lamaze International. Lamaze.org.

Narváez, Darcia. *Neurobiology and the Development of Human Morality: Evolution, Culture, and Wisdom*. New York: W. W. Norton &

Co., 2014.

Neufeld, Gordon, and Gabor Maté. *Hold On to Your Kids: Why Parents Need to Matter More Than Peers.* New York: Ballantine Books, 2006.

Oldfield, Jeremy, Neil Humphrey, and Judith Hebron. "The Role of Parental and Peer Attachment Relationships and School Connectedness in Predicting Adolescent Mental Health Outcomes." *Child and Adolescent Mental Health* 21, no. 1 (May 18, 2015): 21–29.

Ouellet, Marc Cardinal. *Divine Likeness: Toward a Trinitarian Anthropology of the Family.* Grand Rapids, MI: Eerdmans, 2006.

Perrin, Maryanne T., April D. Fogleman, David S. Newburg, and Jonathan C. Allen. "A Longitudinal Study of Human Milk Composition in the Second Year Postpartum: Implications for Human Milk Banking." *Maternal and Child Nutrition* 13, no. 1 (January 2017).

Pennestri, Marie-Hélène, Christine Laganière, Andrée-Anne Bouvette-Turcot, Irina Pokhvisneva, Meir Steiner, Michael J. Meaney, and Hélène Gaudreau. "Uninterrupted Infant Sleep, Development, and Maternal Mood." *Pediatrics* 142, no. 6 (December 2018).

Piazza, Elise A., Liat Hasenfratz, Uri Hasson, and Casey Lew-Williams. "Infant and Adult Brains Are Coupled to the Dynamics of Natural Communication." *Psychological Science* 31, no. 1 (December 17, 2019).

Richter, David, Michael D. Krämer, Nicole K. Y. Tang, Hawley E. Montgomery-Downs, and Sakari Lemola. "Long-Term Effects of Pregnancy and Childbirth on Sleep Satisfaction and Duration of First-Time and Experienced Mothers and Fathers." *Sleep* 42, no. 4 (April 2019).

Yoshida, Sachine, Yoshihiro Kawahara, Takuya Sasatani, Ken Kiyono, Yo Kobayashi, and Hiromasa Funato. "Infants Show Physiological Responses Specific to Parental Hugs." *iScience* 23, no. 4 (April 24, 2020).

Seligman, Martin E. P. *The Optimistic Child: A Proven Program to Safeguard Children Against Depression and Build Lifelong Resilience.* New York: Mariner Books, 2007.

Shivanandan, Mary. *The Holy Family: Model Not Exception.* Glen Echo, MD: KM Associates, 2018.

Siegel, Daniel J. M.D., and Tina Payne Bryson, Ph.D. *The Power of Showing Up: How Parental Presence Shapes Who Our Kids Become and How Their Brains Get Wired*. New York: Ballantine Books, 2020.

Siegel, Daniel J. *The Pocket Guide to Interpersonal Neurobiology: An Integrative Handbook of the Mind*. New York: W. W. Norton, 2012.

Smarius, Laetitia Joanna Clara Antonia, Thea G. A. Strieder, Eva M. Loomans, Theo A. H. Doreleijers, Tanja G. M. Vrijkotte, Reinoud J. Gemke, and Manon van Eijsden. "Excessive Infant Crying Doubles the Risk of Mood and Behavioral Problems at Age 5: Evidence for Mediation by Maternal Characteristics." *European Child & Adolescent Psychiatry* 26, no. 3 (2016): 293–302.

Society for Consumer Psychology. "A New Strategy to Alleviate Sadness: Bring the Emotion to Life: Researchers Show How Characters from the Movie 'Inside Out' Hold the Key to Regulating Emotions and Behavior." ScienceDaily.com, October 3, 2019. https://www.sciencedaily.com/releases/2019/10/191003103515.htm.

US Bureau of Labor Statistics. "Average Hours Per Day Parents Spent Caring for and Helping Household Children as Their Main Activity." American Time Use Survey, accessed November 24, 2020. https://www.bls.gov/charts/american-time-use/activity-by-parent.htm.

Wambach, Karen, and Becky Spencer. *Breastfeeding and Human Lactation*, 6th ed. Burlington, MA: Jones and Bartlett Learning, 2019.

World Health Organization. Child mortality. The Partnership for Maternal, Newborn, and Child Health, https://www.who.int/pmnch/about/en/#.

Notes

Chapter 2

1. Pope Saint John Paul II, Homily, January 28, 1979, http://www.vatican.va/content/john-paul-ii/en/homilies/1979/documents/hf_jp-ii_hom_19790128_messico-puebla-seminario.html.

2. Cardinal Marc Ouellet, *Divine Likeness: Toward a Trinitarian Anthropology of the Family* (Grand Rapids, MI: Eerdmans, 2006).

Chapter 3

1. Pope Francis, *Amoris Laetitia*, March 19, 2016, 87.

2. Barbara H. Fiese, *Family Routines and Rituals* (New Haven, CT: Yale University Press, 2006).

3. Elise Harris, "Eat with Your Family, Not with Your Smartphone, Pope Says," *Catholic News Agency*, November 11, 2015.

4. "This likeness reveals that man, who is the only creature on earth which God willed for itself, cannot fully find himself except through a sincere gift of himself." Pastoral Constitution on the Church in the Modern World, *Gaudium et Spes* (December 7, 1965): 24.

5. Daniel J. Siegel, M.D., and Tina Payne Bryson, Ph.D., *The Power of Showing Up: How Parental Presence Shapes Who Our Kids Become and How Their Brains Get Wired* (New York: Ballantine Books, 2020).

6. Sachine Yoshida, Yoshihiro Kawahara, Takuya Sasatani, Ken Kiyono, Yo Kobayashi, and Hiromasa Funato, "Infants Show Physiological Responses Specific to Parental Hugs," *iScience* 23, no. 4 (April

24, 2020).

Chapter 4

1. Pope Saint John Paul II, *Familiaris Consortio*, 17.

2. Visit Momfidence.org to learn more.

3. Vern L. Bengtson, *Families and Faith: How Religion Is Passed Down across Generations* (Oxford: Oxford University Press, 2017); Darcia Narváez, *Neurobiology and the Development of Human Morality: Evolution, Culture, and Wisdom* (New York: W. W. Norton & Co., 2014).

4. Pope Francis tweet, October 27, 2015.

5. "Workaholic Fathers Are Turning Children into 'Orphans,' Says Francis," *Catholic Herald*, January 28, 2015.

Chapter 5

1. Mary Shivanandan, *The Holy Family: Model Not Exception* (Glen Echo, MD: KM Associates, 2018).

Chapter 6

1. Elżbieta Osewska and Barbara Simonič, "A Civilization of Love according to John Paul II," *The Person and the Challenges* 9, no. 1 (2019): 23–32.

Chapter 7

1. Narváez, *Neurobiology and the Development of Human Morality*. Barbara H. Fiese, *Family Routines and Rituals* (New Haven, CT: Yale University Press, 2006). Vern L. Bengtson, R. David Hayward, Phil Zuckerman, and Merril Silverstein, "Bringing Up Nones: Intergenerational Influences and Cohort Trends," *Journal for the Scientific Study of Religion* 57, no. 2 (June 2018).

2. Mark M. Gray, Ph.D., "The Catholic Family: 21st Century Challenges in the United States," CARA and Holy Cross Family Ministries, June 2015, https://cara.georgetown.edu/staff/webpages/CatholicFamilyResearch.pdf.

3. Bengtson, *Families and Faith*; Justin Bartkus and Christian Smith, *A Report on American Catholic Religious Parenting* (Notre

Dame, IN: McGrath Institute for Church Life, 2015).

4. Gordon Neufeld and Gabor Maté, *Hold On to Your Kids: Why Parents Need to Matter More Than Peers* (New York: Ballantine Books, 2006); Jeremy Oldfield, Neil Humphrey, and Judith Hebron, "The Role of Parental and Peer Attachment Relationships and School Connectedness in Predicting Adolescent Mental Health Outcomes," *Child and Adolescent Mental Health* 21, no. 1 (May 18, 2015).

5. John Bowlby, *A Secure Base: Parent-Child Attachment and Healthy Human Development* (New York: Basic Books, 1999). Mary D. Salter Ainsworth, Mary C. Blehar, Everett Waters, and Sally N. Wall, *Patterns of Attachment: A Psychological Study of the Strange Situation* (New York: Routledge, 2015).

6. Pope John Paul II, *Evangelium Vitae*, March 25, 1995, 93.

7. Philip M. Mamalakis, "Eastern Christian Perspectives on the Church of the Home," in *The Household of God and Local Households: Revisiting the Domestic Church*, eds. Gerard Mannion, Peter De Mey, and Thomas Knieps-Port le Roi (Leuven, Belgium: Peeters, 2013).

8. Louis Cozolino, *The Neuroscience of Human Relationships: Attachment and the Developing Social Brain* (New York: W. W. Norton & Co., 2014); Narváez, *Neurobiology and the Development of Human Morality.*

9. Dr. Tim Clinton and Dr. Gary Sibcy, *Attachments: Why You Love, Feel, and Act the Way You Do* (Nashville: Thomas Nelson, 2009); Dr. Tim Clinton and Dr. Joshua Straub, *God Attachment: Why You Believe, Act, and Feel the Way You Do about God* (Brentwood, TN: Howard Books, 2014).

Chapter 8

1. James W. Fowler, *Stages of Faith: The Psychology of Human Development and the Quest for Meaning* (New York: HarperOne, 1995). Narváez, *Neurobiology and the Development of Human Morality.*

Chapter 9

1. David Richter, Michael D. Krämer, Nicole K. Y. Tang, Hawley E. Montgomery-Downs, and Sakari Lemola, "Long-Term Effects of

Pregnancy and Childbirth on Sleep Satisfaction and Duration of First-Time and Experienced Mothers and Fathers," *Sleep* 42, no. 4, April 2019.

2. Bishop Robert Barron, "Priests, Prophets, Kings," *Word on Fire,* February 14, 2014, https://www.wordonfire.org/resources /article/priests-prophets-kings/477/.

3. Christina Maslach and Michael P. Leiter, "Understanding the Burnout Experience: Recent Research and Its Implications for Psychiatry," *World Psychiatry* 15, no. 2, June 2016.

4. Society for Consumer Psychology, "A New Strategy to Alleviate Sadness: Bring the Emotion to Life," ScienceDaily.com, October 3, 2019, https://www.sciencedaily.com/releases/2019/10/191003103515. htm.

Chapter 10

1. Cozolino, *The Neuroscience of Human Relationships*; Narváez, *Neurobiology and the Development of Human Morality.*

Chapter 14

1. Carol Dwyer, Carol Dweck, and Heather Carlson-Jaquez, "Using Praise to Enhance Student Resilience and Learning Outcomes," American Psychological Association, 2010, https://www.apa.org /education/k12/using-praise.

Chapter 23

1. Martin E. P. Seligman, *The Optimistic Child: A Proven Program to Safeguard Children Against Depression and Build Lifelong Resilience* (Mariner Books, 2007).

2. American Academy of Pediatrics, "American Academy of Pediatrics Announces New Safe Sleep Recommendations to Protect Against SIDS," 2016. http://www.safehealthychildren.org /american-academy-of-pediatrics-announces-new-safe-sleep -recommendations-to-protect-against-sids/

3. "Baby Sleep Expertise Leads to New Bedsharing Advice," Durham University, January 7, 2020, https://www.dur.ac.uk /research/news/item/?itemno=40658.

4. James J. McKenna, Ph.D., *Safe Infant Sleep: Expert Answers to Your Cosleeping Questions* (Washington, DC: Platypus Media, 2020).

5. Kathleen Kendall-Tackett, "Exclusively Breastfeeding Mothers Get More Sleep: Another Look at Nighttime Breastfeeding and Postpartum Depression," *Connecting the Dots* blog, Lamaze International, October 19, 2011, https://www.lamaze.org/Connecting -the-Dots/exclusively-breastfeeding-mothers-get-more-sleep-another -look-at-nighttime-breastfeeding-and-postpartum-depression.

6. Marie-Hélène Pennestri, Christine Laganière, Andrée-Anne Bouvette-Turcot, Irina Pokhvisneva, Meir Steiner, Michael J. Meaney, and Hélène Gaudreau, "Uninterrupted Infant Sleep, Development, and Maternal Mood," *Pediatrics* 142, no. 6 (December 2018).

7. Elise A. Piazza, Liat Hasenfratz, Uri Hasson, and Casey Lew-Williams, "Infant and Adult Brains Are Coupled to the Dynamics of Natural Communication," *Psychological Science* 31, no. 1 (December 17, 2019).

8. C. T. Beck, "Predictors of Postpartum Depression: An Update," *Nursing Research* 50, no. 5 (September–October 2001): 275–85.

Chapter 24

1. American Academy of Pediatrics, "Breastfeeding and the Use of Human Milk," *Pediatrics* 129, no. 3 (March 2012).

2. Jan Barger, "Is It Strange to Still Be Nursing My 2-year-old?" BabyCenter, https://www.babycenter.com/toddler/feeding/is-it -strange-to-still-be-nursing-my-2-year-old_4759#.

3. Mandy Brown Belfort, "The Science of Breastfeeding and Brain Development," *Breastfeeding Medicine* 12, no. 8 (August 2017).

4. Maryanne T. Perrin, April D. Fogleman, David S. Newburg, and Jonathan C. Allen, "A Longitudinal Study of Human Milk Composition in the Second Year Postpartum: Implications for Human Milk Banking," *Maternal and Child Nutrition* 13, no. 1 (January 2017).

5. Wendy Middlemiss, Douglas A. Granger, Wendy A. Goldberg, and Laura Nathans, "Asynchrony of Mother-Infant Hypothalamic-Pituitary-Adrenal Axis Activity Following Extinction of Infant Crying Responses Induced During the Transition to Sleep," *Early*

Human Development 88, no. 4 (April 2012): 227–32.

6. Mayo Clinic Staff, "Chronic Stress Puts Your Health at Risk," Healthy Lifestyle: Stress Management, March 19, 2019, https://www.mayoclinic.org/healthy-lifestyle/stress-management/in-depth/stress/art-20046037.

7. Claire McCarthy, M.D., "New Study Says that It's OK to Let Babies Cry at Night," *Harvard Health Blog*, May 31, 2016, https://www.health.harvard.edu/blog/new-study-says-okay-let-babies-cry-night-201605319774#.

8. L. J. Smarius, T. G. Strieder, E. M. Loomans, T. A. Doreleijers, T. G. Vrijkotte, R. J. Gemke, and M. van Eijsden, "Excessive Infant Crying Doubles the Risk of Mood and Behavioral Problems at Age 5: Evidence for Mediation by Maternal Characteristics," *European Child & Adolescent Psychiatry* 26, no. 3 (July 15, 2016): 293–302.

9. American Academy of Pediatrics, "Parent-child Reading and Story Time Promote Brain Development Prior to Kindergarten," 2014.

Chapter 25

1. Pope Saint John Paul II, *Familiaris Consortio*, 36, 1981.

2. Anna J. Egalite, "How Family Background Influences Student Achievement," *Education Next* 16, no. 2 (February 17, 2016).

3. James W. Fowler, *Stages of Faith* (New York: Harper One, 1995).

Chapter 26

1. Judith Rich Harris, *The Nurture Assumption: Why Children Turn Out the Way They Do*, rev. ed. (New York: Free Press, 2009).

2. Jonah Lehrer, "Do Parents Matter?" *Scientific American*, April 9, 2009, https://www.scientificamerican.com/article/parents-peers-children/#.

3. US Bureau of Labor Statistics, "Average Hours per Day Parents Spent Caring for and Helping Household Children as Their Main Activity," 2018.

4. Gray, "The Catholic Family: 21st Century Challenges in the United States."

5. John Jerrim, Luis Alejandro Lopez-Agudo, and Oscar D. Marcenaro-Gutierrez, "Does It Matter What Children Read? New Evidence Using Longitudinal Census Data from Spain," *Oxford Review of Education* 46, no. 5 (February 27, 2020): 515–33.

About the Authors

Dr. Greg and Lisa Popcak are the authors of more than twenty books and the hosts of More2Life, a call-in advice program airing weekdays on EWTN and SiriusXM 130. Together, they direct CatholicCounselors.com, a Catholic tele-counseling practice serving couples, families, and individuals around the world. In collaboration with Holy Cross Family Ministries, Dr. Greg and Lisa founded the Peyton Institute for Domestic Church Life, which promotes family spirituality and family well-being through professional training and original research. The Popcaks are members of the US Conference of Catholic Bishops' National Advisory Board for Marriage and Family Ministry.

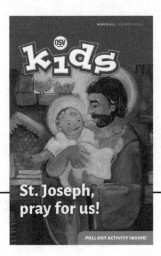

FOR YOUR KIDS

OSV Kids Faithful, fresh, and fun books for children and their families. Parents and grandparents are turning to OSV for the best in children's books from OSV Kids. Each book added to the OSV Kids line is prayerfully considered, from the message, to the artwork, to the production quality and value. Always faithful to the teachings of the Catholic faith, families can trust OSV Kids to help them lead their children to Christ and his Church.

God the Father and the Best Day Ever
By Gracie Jagla, Illustrated by Jacob Popcak
With beautiful illustrations and memorable rhyme, this book tells the sweeping story of God's love for us since the beginning of time. Your child will learn how Jesus' life, death, and resurrection opened heaven, so we can spend eternity with God.

The Wordless Weaver
By Claudia Cangilla McAdam, Illustrated by Caroline Baker Mazure
In this relatable, heartwarming story for children, The Wordless Weaver presents the passion, death, and resurrection of Jesus through the eyes of a child. Filled with beautiful original artwork, this picture book shares the good news of Easter in a way that children will love.

Glory Be Saints A to Z
Rebecca Pohlmeier

Children will learn their ABCs and connect with the saints and their symbols in this adorable board book. While they learn the alphabet and letter sounds, they will also learn to love and respect beloved saints, from Augustine to Zélie. Perfect for gift-giving or to add to your own child's library, Glory Be Saints A to Z is a wonderful way to promote reading readiness and reinforce the Catholic Faith through the lives of the saints.

MORE READING
FOR PARENTS

Parenting Your Teens and Tweens with Grace (Ages 11 to 18)
Dr. Greg and Lisa Popcak

Being a parent of adolescents is tough work. Trying to raise faithful teens and tweens can seem like an impossible mission. Today's Catholic parents need access to the best tools and most up-to-date research to help them fully cooperate with God's grace. That's what Dr. Greg and Lisa Popcak seek to help you do in Parenting Your Teens and Tweens with Grace. Building on their best-selling book Parenting with Grace, first published twenty years ago, this new volume draws on the same parenting principles and provides up-to-date research to guide parents on how to raise preteens and teenagers with grace and joy.